KILLING THE STORY

KILLING
THE STORY

JOURNALISTS RISKING
THEIR LIVES TO UNCOVER
THE TRUTH IN MEXICO

TÉMORIS GRECKO

Translated from the Spanish by Diane Stockwell

THE
NEW
PRESS

NEW YORK
LONDON

Requests for permission to reproduce selections from this book should be made through our website: https://thenewpress.com/contact.

Published in the United States by The New Press, New York, 2020
Distributed by Two Rivers Distribution

ISBN 978-1-62097-502-2 (hc)
ISBN 978-1-62097-503-9 (ebook)
CIP data is available

The New Press publishes books that promote and enrich public discussion and understanding of the issues vital to our democracy and to a more equitable world. These books are made possible by the enthusiasm of our readers; the support of a committed group of donors, large and small; the collaboration of our many partners in the independent media and the not-for-profit sector; booksellers, who often hand-sell New Press books; librarians; and above all by our authors.

www.thenewpress.com

Book design and composition by Bookbright Media
This book was set in Garamond Premier Pro and Gill Sans

Support for this book was generously provided, in part, by FJC—A Foundation of Philanthropic Funds.

Printed in the United States of America

10 9 8 7 6 5 4 3 2 1

Journalism is an insatiable passion that can only be digested and humanized by its brutal confrontation with reality. No one who hasn't suffered it can imagine that servitude that feeds on the unexpected occurrences in life. No one who hasn't lived it can even conceive the supernatural beating of the heart produced by news, the orgasm of having an exclusive, the moral demolition of failure. No one who wasn't born for this and is willing to live only for this could persist in an occupation that is so incomprehensible and voracious, with an oeuvre that is over after every news item, as if it were going to last forever, but that doesn't allow for a moment of peace while it starts all over again, with more ardor than ever in the next minute.

—Gabriel García Márquez

I believe that to do journalism, first of all, you have to be a good man, a good woman: a good human being. Bad people cannot be good journalists. If you are a good person, you can try to understand others, their intentions, their faith, their interests, their problems, their tragedies. And become, immediately, from the first moment, a part of their destiny. This quality is known as "empathy" in psychology. Through empathy, you can understand the character of the speaker and share in a natural, sincere way the fate and the problems of others.

—Ryszard Kapuściński

We shall not cease from exploration
And the end of all our exploring
Will be to arrive where we started
And know the place for the first time.

—T.S. Eliot

CONTENTS

INTRODUCTION

August 1, 2015. That night, we gathered at a colleague's home. Five bodies had been found, murdered execution-style in an apartment in the Narvarte neighborhood of Mexico City. One of them had been a fellow journalist, another a social justice activist. Both had recently fled to the nation's capital in search of safety and were now dead. Our nerves were shattered. Some wept. Not only did anger and sorrow fill the room, but also something approaching panic. We were journalists—reporters, photographers, writers, defenders of the freedom of speech—and we were being murdered. Not even Mexico City could protect us—not our friends, not the organizations launched to support us, nor the Federal Mechanism for the Protection of Human Rights Defenders and Journalists, which had been set up by the government to shield us from the violence. In Mexico, it's not the law that has the long arm but corruption, which operates in the streets and in government offices and executive suites across the country, and it is claiming countless lives across the country.

Everything suggested that the mastermind behind the crime came from outside of the capital—from the state the victims had fled. It was one thing for politicians and their criminal associates to carry out their vendettas in places where the police and prosecutors were in their pay, where protest was quickly silenced. But this was different. We had no doubt that the mayor of Mexico City, Miguel Ángel Mancera, and his staff were corrupt, but not so corrupt they would let themselves be dragged down so low and let him off. They would heed the call for justice or, at the very least, avoid being smeared with other people's shit. Wouldn't they want it known in the nation's capital that they were the ones in charge, that outsiders could not just come in and do whatever they pleased on their turf?

I wanted to believe that the perpetrator of the crime would be held accountable. I wasn't alone. Some of my colleagues told us we were naïve. Territory meant nothing, they said; in our country impunity reigns supreme. Was this just cynicism that made them say this? I was convinced they were wrong. There was much that was wrong with Mexico, my home, but it was nothing like the failed states I had seen as a reporter: Libya, for instance, or Syria, or Somalia. We had not come to that. Or was I wrong?

We were now all in danger. The city had ceased to be a refuge. It was no longer the beacon of freedom that it had been. The message was very clear: none of us were safe. None of us could evade them when they decided to come for us. There was no one to protect us.

I had flown back to Mexico a year earlier for what I thought would be the usual few weeks. The visits home were inevitably short. Every time I returned, it wasn't long before I would feel the tug of far-off corners of the world and return to my nomadic life as a journalist. But, once away from Mexico, I wanted the wonderful food, the music, the mezcal. I wanted to immerse myself in the warm conviviality of my people, their sense of humor, their love of color. I wanted the privilege that most foreign journalists have to take refuge at home from the horrors of war. At the worst times, when bombs were falling around us in Gaza or Libya, even when two of my journalist colleagues and I were taken captive in Syria, I trusted I would get out of there and return to my country. For the almost fourteen years I'd worked as a reporter in some of the most war-torn areas of the world, I believed in that fantasy—I need to. But, as it turned out, it was the privilege of journalists from a different sort than Mexico. Once back in my country, I found myself back in a conflict zone.

My country was being torn apart by violence. Thousands were losing their lives each years. In his documentary *Which Way Is the Front Line from Here?* American journalist Sebastian Junger says, "The ultimate truth about war is not that you might die. The ultimate truth about war is that you are guaranteed to lose your brothers." Journalist brothers, he meant. But to us in Mexico, it wasn't only about the professionals who understood the risks they were taking. It was about people you loved who had no choice but to face death where they live—family, friends, former classmates. In this conflict, there was no use looking for a front line. It was not over here; it wasn't over there; it was everywhere in the vast area of 770,000 square miles where we all lived. There were no clearly identifiable sides, and it was rare that you could clearly identify an enemy—they could be a coworker, or someone walking alongside you on the street; they could run a giant corporation or smile at us from a seat in Congress. And the justice system wasn't geared to dealing with the crisis. Because of corruption and the sheer number of cases it had to deal with, nearly 90 percent of murders do not result in a conviction, according to Mexican organization Zero Impunity.

It wasn't until the murders in Narvarte in July 2015 that I truly understood I was going to be in Mexico for much longer than I'd anticipated. Now was the time to stay and confirm my commitment to my country and to my journalist colleagues who were being murdered for following their calling. But looking back, I may have subconsciously decided earlier, as early as my most recent return a year before, in August 2014, which roughly coincided with two of the most notorious massacres in recent history. Both incidents showed the brutality, the corruption, and the impunity of the authorities involved at their worst.

On June 30, 2014, seven weeks before I returned, the Mexican Army reported a confrontation in the small town of Tlatlaya in Mexico State, which surrounds Mexico City, between a squadron of eight soldiers and a group of twenty-two supposed *sicarios* (hit men), described as members of the criminal organization La Familia Michoacana. The gun battle ended with one soldier wounded, all of the sicarios dead, and the three women who had been abducted safe. At least, that was the official account, but reporters soon found contradictory evidence. Journalists for the Associated Press "found little evidence of a long gun battle. Instead, the walls showed a repeated pattern of one or two closely placed bullet holes surrounded by spattered blood, giving the appearance that some of those killed had been standing against a wall and shot at about chest level." Their suspicions were confirmed when journalists Pablo Ferri and Nathalie Iriarte managed to locate an eyewitness, who told them that only one of the twenty-two victims had been killed in the shootout. The other twenty-one had been executed in cold blood, their bodies arranged to look like they had died in a gun fight.

Numerous attempts were made to discredit the journalists, but the National Human Rights Commission confirmed that at least fifteen people had been executed in the incident. Three low-ranking soldiers who had allegedly been involved were then prosecuted (and later acquitted). And that was it. No officers would be investigated. No one would try to find out who had tampered with the crime scene. No commanders responsible for securing the perimeter of the scene were questioned. No one would review the orders given that day or the rules of engagement. No one would find out if similar incidents had taken place that might indicate a pattern of similar strategies.

Months later, the country was rocked by another act of violence. On the night and morning of September 26 and 27 in the city of Iguala in the southern state of Guerrero, more than one hundred students from the rural education college Escuela Normal Rural de Ayotzinapa, and other civilians who happened to be in the area, were attacked by gunmen and municipal police officers working for the Guerreros Unidos crime group and harassed by state and federal police, as well as the military, while in need of urgent medical attention—even as the extensive operation was monitored and reported in real time by military intelligence.

Six people were killed, twenty-five were wounded, a young man suffered severe brain damage, and forty-three college students were forcibly disappeared. Hijacking buses to get to a demonstration in Mexico City—a common practice—the students had accidentally commandeered a vehicle that carried a hidden heroin cargo valued at millions of dollars, and the owner of the drugs had ordered them to be stopped at any cost. The case rocked the country, causing a wave of large-scale protests demanding that the students be found alive before it was too late.

Weeks passed, and the protests only intensified. The state and federal authorities didn't invest their resources in a thorough, transparent investigation. For them, finding the students, dead or alive, was risky: after all, it might turn out not to be just a local matter, confined to a few municipalities. The students might have been caught up in a transnational heroin trafficking network that not only implicated local authorities but state and federal civil and military authorities as well. Over the years, people had discovered hundreds of bodies of people who had been abducted and tossed into clandestine graves in the hills, but any attempt to bring attention to them resulted in silence, if not reprisals. This time looked no different.

In November, Mexico's attorney general Jesús Murillo Karam announced the preliminary results of the investigation, pointing the finger firmly at the mayor of Iguala, who had links to the Guerreros Unidos. Murillo Karam claimed that only local police had been involved—not the army or the federal police, who, according to Karam, only found out about it hours later, even though their headquarters were along the route where the students had been pursued, and the local security communications center, which is under military control, had reported on events as they happened. And there had been no reason to intervene. The legal obligation of the military and the federal police was not to protect unarmed civilians under attack but to support the authorities. So went Murillo Karam's account.

And where were the forty-three? Murillo Karam said they had

all been taken to a remote trash dump in the neighboring municipality of Cocula, where six gang members had killed them. Their
bodies were then incinerated in a giant bonfire made from scav-
enged trash and wood. As evidence, Murillo Karam presented a
bone fragment he said had been identified as belonging to one of
the students. And that was it. No clothing, no hair, no cell phones.
No more identifiable bones. The killers on that rainy night had
built a fire as hot as an industrial oven that it could incinerate all
traces of DNA over the course of fifteen hours.

Both of these massacres occurred under the presidency of Enrique
Peña Nieto, seriously undermining his government's credibility.
When I began writing this book, he was almost halfway through
his six-year term. He had been trained as a lawyer at the Roman
Catholic Opus Dei–backed Panamerican University and earned
a master's degree in business administration from the elite Tecnológico de Monterrey. A close relative to two former governors
of Mexico State, he was given the governorship—one of the most
important in the country—without any experience in elected
office or public administration. A widowed father, he had the
bland good looks of a soap opera star, and he needed a partner
to bolster his image. Grupo Televisa, with its four national television channels, would provide strong support in promoting Peña
Nieto's candidacy and offered up one of their leading actresses to
fill the role of First Lady: Angélica Rivera, known as "La Gaviota"
for a soap opera character she played.

Peña Nieto was presented as the reformer president, and people
lapped it up. Major media outlets stopped talking about a country
drenched in blood and started promoting a message of promise

and renovation. This great nation, which had kicked off the new millennium sluggishly, was finally ready to get going.

The president was a member of the Institutional Revolutionary Party (PRI), which for seventy-one years, from 1929 until 2000, had ruled the country. It was essentially a one-party hegemony, with a token opposition party, the National Action Party (PAN), in the wings; all other political organizations were satellite parties to the PRI. The political culture that evolved under the PRI was hierarchical—a system of patronage that allowed corruption, hypocrisy, and nepotism to flourish. It was also a system in which the ties between the media and ruling elite were tight, and there were all sorts of unspoken rules about what journalists should and should not say about the ruling party or public officials. There were also various ways by which the government rewarded and punished the media; most importantly, perhaps, the lucrative advertising contracts to publications that provide favorable coverage—a vital source of revenue for the media. Many newspapers accepted payments to include official announcements that were thinly disguised as editorials.

It was only at the turn of the millennium that PRI's rule came to an end, when PAN won the 2000 elections and Vicente Fox assumed the presidency. In reality little changed. PAN, considered socially conservative and economically neoliberal, and the PRI, which also favored a neoliberal economy, both represented the interests of the multimillionaire business elites, transnational corporations, and foreign investors, and they had a similar relationship with the media. On the left was the Party of the Democratic Revolution (PRD), and there were also six smaller parties (known as *la chiquillada*), each with a vague ideological platform, that managed to survive by forming alliances with the three larger parties. Yet the PRI political culture remained and was further consolidated when the PRI returned to power in 2012 with the victory of Peña Nieto as president.

The opposition was led, just as it had been for a decade, by Andrés Manuel López Obrador (AMLO), who had been mayor of Mexico City from 2000 to 2005. Running on a platform of fighting corruption and the "power mafia" of political and economic elites, AMLO has managed to set the political agenda for years, with his sustained popularity and the animosity of foes who have tried to impede his access to power. López Obrador ran for president in 2006, and, according to his supporters, it was only electoral fraud that had kept him from winning, with official figures reporting he lost to his opponent Felipe Calderón by just half a percent. Almost immediately, Peña Nieto began preparing his own campaign, crafting an informal cross-party alliance—an operation launched to guarantee benefits for Mexico's elites—where television played a fundamental role in selling him to voters. Peña Nieto defeated López Obrador in 2012, but by only 6 percent, according to official figures.

Ever the non-conformist, López Obrador condemned the support that his party, the PRD, gave the new president by signing the Pact for Mexico, which brought all the parties together under one umbrella. He then proceeded to lead the defection of thousands of mostly working- and middle-class citizens angered by pervasive corruption and impunity in the government, forming the MORENA (National Regeneration Movement) party. Through the new party, he was mounting his next challenge to the system as I returned to Mexico, and by the time I finished this book, Peña

Nieto, once so popular but now widely derided and tainted by scandal, was out, and AMLO was president.

Two months into his presidency, López Obrador declared an end to the country's militarized war on drugs. "There is no war on drugs, officially, there is no war. We want peace, we are going to get peace. . . . The principal mission of the government is to guarantee public security." Regardless of the efficacy of his policies in reducing violence in the country, it is one of the clearest signals that the new president was breaking with his predecessors and the prevailing rhetoric of the war on organized crime that had started under President Felipe Calderón. When PAN's Felipe Calderón won the presidency in 2006, he was dogged by claims of electoral fraud and needed a major initiative to give his presidency legitimacy. At the time, daily news of "cartel violence" seemed to show a country near conquered by organized criminal groups. Assuring the public that the crisis was so severe that extreme measures had to be taken to contain it, he declared a war on drugs, and to fight it, he brought in the military. Tens of thousands of army and navy personnel took to the streets, but it never seemed to rein in the violence. The effect was quite the opposite. The policy of targeting the heads of organized criminal groups, of taking down their kingpins, which was continued by his successor, Peña Nieto, led to brutal internecine fighting and to new competing groups, some of them breaking off from larger groups. Meanwhile, the police and the military ended up killing thousands of people they alleged to be criminals.

Were we really in a crisis of violence? Was organized crime out of control? Were there more murders than ever? Data on deaths by homicide from the National Institute of Statistics and Geography showed that between 1960 and 2007, when Mexico had a population of 38 million (a third of today's), there was a downward trend. In 1995, for every 100,000 inhabitants there were 16.9 homicides; in 2000, 10.8; and in 2007, the first year of Calderón's war, there were 8.2: half the number from twelve years earlier. The index in 2008 was 50 percent greater than the previous year: 12.9. In 2009 it went up another 50 percent, to 17.7, surpassing the figure from 1995. It took Calderón only two years to erase the gains made in the past twelve. But it kept getting worse. In 2017, the last year of Peña Nieto's term, there were 25.3 homicides for every 100,000 residents in Mexico. Figures from the close of 2018 show an increase of 15 percent over the previous year, from 28,886 to 33,341 victims. Never before in the nation's history, since crimes had been recorded, had so many people been killed.

The prevailing view in Mexico and the United States, promoted by both governments and uncritically echoed by most journalists, is that we are at war, and the Mexican state must battle "narco-trafficking cartels" so powerful they are practically invincible, obliging us all to support every decision made by the authorities and admit their abuses as collateral damage. We must spend whatever it takes to deploy police and military personnel and accept the inevitable consequences: the torture, the killings, the massacres, not only by organized criminal groups but also by the police and the military, who are often quick to shoot anyone suspected of criminal activity.

It's vital to remain circumspect about how this "war" is portrayed. It's all too easy to refer to cartels and narco-trafficking. For a start, these groups are not, strictly speaking, cartels, and many of these groups are involved in a variety of activities, not just the trafficking of illegal drugs, which can be just a side business for them. "Cartels don't exist," a lawyer for alleged members of the Medellin Cartel Gustavo Salazar said to British journalist Ioan Grillo. "What you have is a collection of drug traffickers. Sometimes they work together, and sometimes they don't. American prosecutors just call them cartels to make it easier to make their cases. It is all part of the game." In this book, I refer to them as criminal organizations or groups or gangs, and only use the word "cartel" when it's part of their widely used name or the way they call themselves, adopting the official terminology. More importantly, the mythology of narco-trafficking, and therefore the prioritization of national security, has had an insidious effect on the collective imagination, one that has helped to neutralize popular opposition. It has been used to distract from other issues, including abysmal deficiencies in education and health care, the widening gap between rich and poor, and the state's attempt to depopulate land, neutralize popular resistance, and facilitate for corporations the mass appropriation of natural resources and the exploitation of labor. Our nation is being sacked without us even turning around to see it, and it is for journalism to clear the smokescreen.

The irony is that a significant part of the profession—traditional media outlets with the largest audiences and readerships—have acted as a cog in the deception machine because of their refusal to criticize and investigate, their penchant for reproducing statements from politicians and officials without comment, their patience for copying and publishing official bulletins and documents (there are columnists who do nothing more than receive official files that "get to them," and faithfully translate them into the language of the press as if they were their own findings, even though they occasionally pretend to be sharp critics of the corruption of the judicial system, separate from their own), and their shameful, but profitable docility. "By favoring some categories and patterns of perception over others with no critical distance, under the pretext of factual objectivity, they adopt the same political, ethical, and esthetic position as those they are appropriating from," according to Universidad Nacional Autónoma de México professor Luis Astorga.

In his book *Narcoperiodismo/Narcojournalism*, Sinaloa-based journalist Javier Valdez Cárdenas described Mexico as a country "where the economic interests of some are placed above the grand majority and [those in power] impose their law with impunity, assassinations, corruption, elections plundering, kidnappings and bribes, all ruthless to the journalists who search for the truth." Every year reporters continue to be killed. No fewer than twenty-two journalists were killed during Vicente Fox's presidency; forty-seven under his successor, Felipe Calderón; the same figure with Enrique Peña Nieto's; and the pace has remained steady under López Obrador's. And, as Valdez wrote, "It is not only the narcos who disappear and kill photographers, editors, and journalists. The job is also done by politicians, police, agents colluding with organized crime, prosecutors, government, and army officials." While some crime groups or public officials bribe journalists for favorable coverage, others use threats or violence to pressure journalists not to expose their crimes or to retaliate against journalists who report on their crimes. They harass, attack, torture, and kill reporters. They sue them; publicly denounce their work; monitor their movements and communications; bomb their offices; and menace their family and friends. And in almost all cases, the intellectual authors of these crimes are never identified, found, or tried. In Mexico, "it is dangerous to be alive, and to do journalism is to walk on an invisible line drawn by the bad guys—who are in drug trafficking and in the government—in a field strewn with explosives," Valdez said as he accepted the International Press Freedom Award in New York in 2011. "This is what most of the country is living through. One must protect oneself from everything and everyone, and there do not seem to be options for salvation, and often there is no one to turn to."

The death toll for journalists in Mexico varies according to the methodology used. For example, the National Human Rights Commission calculates that 141 journalists were assassinated between 2000 and 2018, while the human rights organization Article 19 Mexico claims it's 121. The National Human Rights Commission is among the groups that maintain that all journalist killings should be included in the registry, independent of the motive. Unsurprisingly, some citizens feel an unnecessary distinction is being made based on the profession, as if the lives of reporters were somehow worth more than everyone else's. Article 19 Mexico documents assassinations committed "in possible relation to their work as journalists": when the victim covered a subject or investigated a matter that someone wanted to cover up with their death. Some of us believe special attention should be paid to crimes committed to prevent information from reaching the public or to punish those who report it. Journalists are the eyes, ears, and mouth of a society that the powerful want to keep blind, deaf, and mute. That is how organizations like Reporters Without Borders and the Committee to Protect Journalists see it.[1]

One of the reasons why little to no progress has been made is the degree to which corruption has infiltrated the criminal justice system at all levels. "The state doesn't investigate itself. There is a direct link between the level of impunity and corruption," Ana Cristina Ruelas, Article 19's director for Mexico and Central America, told the BBC. "This impunity allows the aggressors to continue attacking the press in broad daylight."[2]

Mexico is a media powerhouse in Latin America, covering an enormous range of outlets from well-established newspapers such as *El Universal* and *Excélsior* to newer websites such as Aristegui Noticias, Sin Embargo, and Animal Político; from Latin America's largest media group Televisa and national networks of TV Azteca to the recently launched Imagen Televisión; from the beacon of independent journalism, the weekly *Proceso,* to new right- and left-wing outlets like *ContraRéplica* and *Desinformémonos.* The vast majority of reporters who have been killed, however, do not work for the national media but for relatively small-scale local media in states dominated by organized crime and political corruption, where, with the collusion of politics and journalists and the silencing of dissenting voices through intimidation and fear, there are few other outlets of investigative reporting on corruption and crime. They have been the most targeted journalists.

As my colleague John Gibler put it, in Mexico, it's more dangerous to investigate a murder than to commit one. Yearly, Mexico ranks among the five countries where the most reporters are killed. The others are usually Syria, Afghanistan, Somalia, and

Iraq. But Mexico is not like them, we are assured. Mexico has functioning democratic institutions, laws, a president who expresses an unwavering commitment to freedom of expression and says he is a friend and ally of a free press. Moreover, Mexico has federal agencies created with the sole purpose of protecting journalists.

In 2006, President Vicente Fox appointed Mexico's first prosecutor to investigate crimes against journalists, and in 2010 the Office of the Special Prosecutor for Crimes Against Freedom of Expression (FEADLE) was created to prosecute crimes against members of the media. In June 2012, the government passed a law for the protection of journalists and human rights activists, and months later it established a federal protection mechanism in the ministry of the interior, the Federal Mechanism for the Protection of Human Rights Defenders and Journalists, to provide bodyguards, panic buttons, and other forms of protection to journalists and activists who were in need of help. The General Victims' Law was passed in 2013, creating a registry of victims of organized crime and a compensation fund for victims and their families. The law gave medical, legal, financial, and psychological support and access to justice for victims of crimes. But, marred by delays and scant resources, among other factors, none of these measures have had an impact on the rate at which journalists are being killed. FEADLE's rate of success from 2010 to 2018, according to Article 19 Mexico's February 2019 report, is 0.87 percent: out of 1,140 investigations, it achieved 10 convictions. Journalists who work in risky areas are forced to improvise their own security measures to protect themselves, such as publishing anonymously, changing daily routines and routes, keeping a low profile, reporting in groups, or even changing location and place of residence.

What the authorities say bears little relation to what they do. Peña Nieto and the state governors spoke passionately about defending freedom of expression while doing little to prevent attacks on the journalists. They have blood on their hands.

Many of my colleagues have dedicated themselves to finding ways of protecting journalists here. In 2007, some journalists joined together to create the Red de Periodistas de a Pie in 2007, a grassroots network focused on professional training and security and on reporting on social justice issues. It became an organizational model followed in many states, where journalists set up their own regional networks. In Mexico City, a number of reporters, photographers, filmmakers, authors, and musicians decided to establish their own collective, and on November 27, 2014, we formed Ojos de Perro vs. la Impunidad.

For one of our projects, we traveled around the country to learn about the places where journalists were being attacked, and interviewed those who were at risk, who had been threatened or hurt, as well as the friends, family, and colleagues of those who were lost. This book stems from that project. Of course, I cannot hope to be comprehensive or to do justice to the work of every journalist putting his or her life on the line for their work, but in these pages you will meet journalists from different backgrounds, from self-trained local journalists to nationally renowned journalists with substantial platforms. Some lost their lives in the pursuit of truth; others survived to hold the perpetrators accountable. If those who died were aware of the risks and decided to pursue their vocation regardless, others have followed, and will follow, in their footsteps. These are courageous women and men who choose not to surrender and who every day reaffirm their commitment to society and who go out to report on crime and corruption despite the dangers, despite the length to which people will go to kill the story. This is not a book without hope. It is a book of resistance. It is a testament to my colleagues' continued heroism. It is dedicated to those who died and to those who are in the struggle.

The truth cannot be killed by killing journalists.

I

Rubén Espinosa I

On the morning of Saturday, August 1, 2015, Itzamná was waiting for Rubén in the city of Puebla, about two hours east of Mexico City. She and Rubén had planned to visit her parents that weekend, and they had arranged to meet beforehand. The last she had heard from him was the day before, and after a restless night, "like when you have that sixth sense telling you something's wrong and you don't know what's going on," she decided to call his sister Alma in Mexico City. He had been staying with her and so she figured Alma might know if he was on his way. Alma checked his room, where she found his camera and all his things still there.

The family began to worry. Rubén's father said he had heard about a multiple homicide the night before, which seemed "very strange because that kind of thing doesn't happen here." This level of violence was thought to belong to other parts of the country—not Mexico City. The family contacted Rubén's other sister Patricia, who was on vacation with her boyfriend in Laguna de Tamiahua on the Gulf of Mexico. They immediately cut short their trip and headed back to Mexico City as quickly as they could.

In the meantime, Alma had managed to get in touch with Arturo, an old friend, who had been with Rubén the night before he disappeared. Arturo explained he and Rubén had gone out on Thursday night for a drink with their activist friend, Nadia Vera, in the city center. After the bar closed for the night, the three had gone back to Nadia's apartment in Colonia Narvarte to continue talking over another beer. They stayed there for the night. Arturo left the apartment on Friday in the early afternoon. Rubén had planned to leave a little later to drop by the local office of AVC Noticias, the Veracruz news agency he worked with. He had also promised his sister Patricia that he would stay at her house that night to take care of her dogs while she was away.

A photographer friend who had been keeping tabs on Rubén to make sure he was safe did not know where he was. He was the last person to have had any contact with him. They had exchanged messages on WhatsApp around two on Friday afternoon, and everything had been fine. He'd asked Rubén what he'd got up to the night before.

"I went out with an old buddy and another friend, I stayed over at her place and I'm just leaving to go to my place now," he replied. "Dude, I'll text you when I get home, I'm going now." It was 2:13 p.m.

Almost twenty-four hours later, there had been no word from him. Around three o'clock, Alma headed to the address Arturo had given her, where he and Rubén and Nadia had gone after the bar: 1909 Calle Luz Saviñón, Apartment 401, in Narvarte. There, she found the area closed off and under police control. She was told that a multiple homicide had taken place in the building, and she knew instinctively her brother had been one of the victims. She started to cry. Police officers told her to stop: maybe he wasn't dead, they said, and insinuated that he was a suspect .

The police took her to the morgue. She said she went in as if in a dream and was suddenly faced with five dead bodies: all completely naked, all but one battered and bruised, almost black. Among them was Rubén.

Rubén was a familiar sight on the streets of Veracruz's capital, Xalapa. Of medium build, with a short beard, he usually wore sunglasses and loose, baggy pants with big pockets, and he always had his camera with him. Rubencillo to his friends and family, he was known to be friendly and laid back, a deeply caring person who would come to the aid of anyone, a friend, a relative, or a colleague, if they were in trouble. "There are many, many people who love him, and even more who trust him," his friend Arantxa Arcos, who is also a reporter, told me.

Born in 1983 in Mexico City, Rubén was raised in the nation's capital in an apartment building at the corner of avenidas Revolución and José Martí, right where the middle-class neighborhood Escandón meets Tacubaya, a grittier area that was the stomping grounds of Los Panchitos, the most notorious street gang at the time.

Rubén taught himself photography. From an early age, he knew it was his calling. In 2006, at twenty-three, he decided to move to the port city of Veracruz to pursue a career as a photographer. Three years later, now in Xalapa, he was hired by politician Javier Duarte de Ochoa to document his gubernatorial campaign. That was followed by a stint working for Elizabeth Morales in her campaign to become the mayor of Xalapa. In a profession where reporters lack social security and usually earn salaries of only 2,000 to 6,000 pesos a month—the equivalent of $110 to $330—where journalists are pressured to accept gifts from government officials and risk getting killed just for doing their work, a job in the public sector can be a very attractive option.

But Rubén's heart was not in it. He quickly tired of the politicians and their machinations and became one of their critics, trading the security of a steady paycheck for the insecurity and freedom of freelancing. He had a passion for social justice, which made him stand out from many of his colleagues. According to his sister Patricia, he was drawn to journalism because he wanted "to show the people the truth, the reality, not to hide it, so they know where we are, what's happening, what is actually going on." His reputation grew. He trained his lens on social activism and the repression of popular protest in the region, and the high quality of Rubén's work meant he was soon contributing to the national weekly news magazine *Proceso* and the agency Cuartoscuro in Mexico City, and the local Veracruz news service AVC Noticias. And it wasn't long before this brought him in conflict with his former employer, now the governor of Veracruz, Javier Duarte.

In Mexico, the thirty-one state governors who, like the president, are elected to six-year terms, rule over their states like lords over their fiefdoms. Previously, under the PRI from 1929 to 2000, their actions were responsible only to the president, but the shift in power to the PAN party in 2000 weakened the power of the federal government over the governors. When Duarte assumed the governorship of Veracruz in 2010, he effectively reigned supreme.

Duarte was born into wealth. His father, Javier Duarte Franco, was a cattle farmer, who died in Mexico City in the famous Hotel Regis when it collapsed during the 1985 earthquake. Javier attended prestigious schools and universities in Mexico City and Madrid, emerging with a doctorate in economics from the Universidad Complutense in Madrid. He worked a variety of jobs, none of which seemed to meet his expectations or his ambitions, and in 1997 he joined the staff of Governor Fidel Herrera, the PRI governor of Veracruz from 2004 until 2010. There he was tasked with scouring the daily newspapers early every morning for the most noteworthy stories, cutting them out of the paper with scissors, and pasting them onto sheets of paper. Loyalty, more than talent, was a key asset, and it allowed him to reach the top, inheriting the position from Herrera. Herrera had calculated that he could still wield power after he left office through one of his meekest underlings—a far from unusual, although not always successful, practice in Mexican politics, as illustrated by what happened next.

Once he came to power in 2010, Duarte severed ties with his predecessor. He rid the PRI and the state of all influence by the former governor and established his own dominion. He sought out every possible means to bolster his self-image and suppress dissent, and any criticisms or jibes only provoked violent reactions from him. Some psychologists who have analyzed Duarte's personality point out a lack of empathy and high levels of insecurity, and they believe his ascension to the governor's office imbued him with a sense of invulnerability and self-confidence, at least on the surface.[1] To take just one example, when asked what historical figure he identified with the most, he compared his curiously high-pitched tenor to that of the brutal Spanish dictator Francisco Franco: "Many people point it out as a defect, but I'm very happy with my voice, my voice identifies me and I really feel very comfortable with it. Franco had the same tone of voice as me," which reflected "strength, enthusiasm, energy."[2]

The third-largest state in population, Veracruz occupies a strategic position in the country, with its long shoreline along the Gulf of Mexico, its major ports on the Atlantic Ocean, and its large oil fields. Many of the smuggling routes used by organized crime groups to transport drugs to the United States traverse its borders. Organized crime had flourished under Herrera, when the crime syndicate known as Los Zetas expanded throughout the state, moving in around the cities of Veracruz, Boca del Río, and Medellín. In addition to trafficking drugs and stealing gasoline, they also made money from kidnapping, racketeering, and extortion.[3] The police did not try to stop them, and in fact, police officers were complicit, harassing business owners, workers, and residents themselves. While in office Herrera was frequently accused of acting in complicity with criminal organizations and his reputation for corruption outlasted his time in office. In October 2015, when he was appointed Mexico's consul general in Barcelona, Barcelona's city council as well as Taula per Mèxic—a Mexican human rights group in Barcelona—complained to Spanish authorities. Herrera had to resign from the diplomatic post just fifteen months later while under criminal investigation for purchasing counterfeit medicines for children undergoing chemotherapy.[4]

The local press had already been under siege during Herrera's term, but the situation took a turn for the worse after Duarte's election. Four journalists had been killed between 2004 and 2010, under Herrera. Other states—Chihuahua, Guerrero, and Tamaulipas—had much higher murder rates for journalists, but Veracruz began to take the lead in 2010, six months after Duarte became governor. During his six-year term, seventeen journalists were killed, and three disappeared.[5]

A watershed moment, both in Veracruz and across the nation in terms of bringing attention to the extraordinary dangers faced by journalists in the state, was the murder of Regina Martínez. On April 28, 2012, the forty-eight-year-old correspondent for *Proceso*, was found tortured and strangled to death in her home in Xalapa.

Born in the mountain town of Rafael Lucio, half an hour from the state capital, Regina had spent her career investigating the corruption of mayors, political candidates, and government officials, as well as suspicious deaths, alleged suicides, and numerous cases of fraud in Veracruz. She had even dared to investigate the army, bringing to light the murder of Ernestina Ascencio Rosario, an elderly indigenous woman who had been brutally raped and killed by soldiers in 2007.

An official investigation into Regina's death was launched. Suspects were identified, an arrest was made, and by its close, Duarte's prosecutors had concluded that an HIV-positive male sex worker named José Hernández and his friend Jorge Hernández (no relation) were the killers. Regina had allegedly fallen in love with José and invited him and his friend over to have some beers. They had taken the opportunity to kill her and steal her laptop, a flat-screen TV, two cell phones, and a camera. People who knew her said that this was entirely out of character. She had been very reserved and would never have behaved like that, but the prosecutors argued that she had changed. They claimed that some cosmetics and perfumes found in her home had acted as an "external agent," making her behave "more enthusiastically" than usual. The district attorney's conclusions were based on the confession of the only person arrested for the murder, Jorge Hernández, who was sentenced to thirty-eight years in prison. (The whereabouts of her alleged lover remain unknown.) Jorge later stated that he had been forced to memorize and confess a version of events that matched that of the authorities. "When they arrested me," he said, "they put electric charges on me, they blindfolded me, they put water up my nose and told me they were going to kill me, and my mother, too."[6]

Regina was not the only journalist to be killed that week. Five days after she was murdered, on May 3, three crime reporters and an administrative staffer at the VeracruzNews agency were murdered by organized criminal groups, for reasons that have never become clear. Israel Hernández, a young reporter for Imagen del Golfo, later took me to the site where the four dismembered bodies were found in black trash bags. They had been thrown into La Zamorana, a putrid canal filled with foul wastewater that empties into the Gulf of Mexico. It was not an isolated site: this was where the three municipalities of Veracruz, Boca del Río, and Medellín meet, right by a middle-class residential development called Las Vegas. "The discovery was made in broad daylight," Israel said. "It was a message that they were in charge and nothing could stop them, and they had the power to do whatever they wanted to whoever they wanted."

Rubén was one of a group of activists who publicly demanded justice for Regina's murder. He would do the same for other journalists, including notably Gregorio Jiménez, a journalist who had been reporting out of Villa Allende, near the city of Coatzacoalcos in Veracruz. His body was found in February 2014, beheaded and with the tongue cut out, buried in a shallow grave with an unidentified taxi driver and a local union leader whose abduction Jiménez had reported on the month before. Rubén was all too aware that, despite the existence official government protections, independent journalists had to take their safety into their own hands, and in 2015, Rubén joined reporters Norma Trujillo (*La Jornada Veracruz*) and Noé Zavaleta (*Proceso*) and videographer Raziel Roldán (*Plumas Libres*) at the café Espresso 58, just two blocks from the government palace in Xalapa, and along with some other colleagues, they formed the collective Voz Alterna, a sanctuary for independent journalism in Xalapa.

Rubén defended all journalists, but not all journalism, or what passes for journalism in Mexico after two centuries in which politicians had such a tight grip over the media. While the concept of journalistic independence has become more widely understood, reporters have had to confront vigorous resistance in the form of boycotts, reprisals, abuse, and forced resignations. Meanwhile, many journalists believe that the journalists' stock-in-trade is to toe the party line and flatter the powerful and that those who do should not be blamed—that they're just doing their job. They think it isn't their place to call out the failures and misdeeds of their colleagues. They mistakenly believe that the dishonesty and corruption of a few journalists do not endanger the journalists who refuse to be corrupted, and that if they submit to power, they are not implicitly damning those who stand up to it.

Voz Alterna directs its criticism not only at external enemies of a free press but also at those who weaken it from within. Rubén learned from his own day-to-day experience that the low salaries and unprotected status of reporters was an effective way to control information. "A reporter in Veracruz could not support a family," he explained in an interview on the television show *Periodistas de a Pie*. "Some of my colleagues work two jobs, and some as many as six."[7]

The reality did nothing to soften their denunciations against journalists who groveled for the smallest crumbs that came their way. From media owners who compromise their editorial integrity in exchange for advertising and business opportunities, to the dinners and breakfasts provided to journalists on World Press Freedom Day by governors, mayors, and their deputies, the suppression of information is rewarded with cars, cash, and gifts of food, drink, and electronics for reporters who put financial desperation or some other motive before doing the right thing.

"In Veracruz, the media are in the service of money, of corruption," Rubén told *Periodistas de a Pie*. "And I'm not just talking about the higher-ups—reporters and photographers, too. They fight over forty-five-peso [$2.50] breakfasts. They'd fight over a plate of food, saying 'they brought it to me, they brought it to me,' when the governor had his breakfasts. We're talking about something really sad. It's a kind of information prostitution that's devastating for society."

This dependence on and obedience to political and economic power concerned Rubén greatly: "The dilemma of telling new journalists there are two kinds of reporters: the ones who sell themselves, who act as a mouthpiece for the government, collect several salaries, and are always going out to fancy dinners. They have nice homes, cars. They throw parties, go on vacations. Then you have the other kind, those of us who want to portray reality, but our pay is low. We get no privileges, no gifts, no meaningless prizes. You'll be compensated in the form of threats, persecution, and death, even your family's."[8]

Salaries are, in fact, an ongoing issue in the profession—at least for those who haven't sold out. They are, for the most part, extremely low, and on top of that any expenses incurred by their work—cameras, phones, cars, gas—usually come out of the journalists' own pockets. According to one journalist I spoke to, the best-paid staff reporters earn around eight thousand pesos a month, but the ones at news agencies don't earn any more than three thousand pesos, and they must write multiple articles per day: "And with the social media boom, now they don't just ask for a story, they want photos and video, too. For the same pay." By contrast, when covering organized crime, which cost him his life, Gregorio Jiménez earned between twenty and forty-five pesos for each article published in small local publications.[9] In major cities the pay is higher, but it's hardly better because of the higher cost of living, and of late freelancers have only seen their rates fall.

If that weren't enough, independent journalist also have to face criticism from their fellow reporters who have sold out. In corrupt circles, people who refuse to participate are seen as the weak link. They could uncover everyone's involvement, illuminating the others' lack of honesty and integrity. They are seen as a threat and are persecuted for it. Rubén denounced "the fight of the press against the press," the journalists who allowed themselves be used by those in power to attack others who refuse to do so. Rubén said, "They call us guerrillas," derogatively, for defending freedom of expression "and for taking responsibility for our own safety. For even the most basic things: wearing a helmet, using gas masks, making maps, the basic things that everybody should know how to do."

This emphasis on personal safety is understandable when faced with the repressive atmosphere in Veracruz. When Rubén was interviewed on *Periodistas de a Pie*, Duarte had been governor for four years, and his power rested on two pillars. One was his press chief, former journalist Gina Domínguez, who purchased favorable, if fictitious, stories about the governor from some reporters while threatening and persecuting reporters who did not follow the party line. She called media directors and issued orders, effectively saying: "[This person] should get this coverage, in this section, with this many words, and under this headline. I want you to run this photo, and it should be under this reporter's byline," journalist Ignacio Carvajal explained. If anyone asked Duarte any uncomfortable questions, Domínguez would demand that the reporter be replaced. To her, public advertising contracts were "editorial alliances," and they could be terminated at any moment if she thought her authority wasn't respected, while those who got with the program and promoted a positive image of the governor were rewarded.[10]

The other pillar supporting Duarte was the secretary of public security, Arturo Bermúdez, who oversaw the police, used uniformed and plainclothes officers to crush any kind of protest or dissent, and severely curtailed what journalists could do. There have been accusations against the state police in at least eighty disappearances between December 2010 and August 2016, where people detained by the police have gone missing.

Bermúdez, who was responsible for protecting the residents of Veracruz, had a particular fondness for violence. Around the world, governments have developed their own repressive techniques that don't kill but leave indelible marks on their citizens.

In Palestine, for example, Israeli water cannons shoot a liquid so noxious, if it splatters on your clothes, you have to throw them away, and you feel compelled to shave off every last hair on your body. The tear gas in Egypt is among the worst anywhere, and those affected have to be dragged to safety, drool pouring from their mouths, eyes rolled back in their heads. In Iran, they send out motorcycle squadrons, with two people riding on each: one to drive and run people over, while his partner delivers kicks and punches. Duarte and Bermúdez preferred electric cattle prods. Under their orders, the riot squad would advance with their prods on the young and the old, the strong and weak, men, women, and children, who screamed as they were zapped with thousands of volts of electricity. Numerous protests have ended this way, whether the protesters were teachers defending their jobs or retirees protesting the government's failure to pay their pensions.

Killings, kidnappings, extortions, and racketeering were widespread in Veracruz, but that did not interest Duarte, Bermúdez, and Domínguez, who instead focused their efforts on silencing the recalcitrant press. The Veracruz version of omertà, the mafia code of silence, was imposed by the government and by criminal organizations, and obeyed by most local media. But there were some who resisted, who helped bring the attention of the rest of the country to what was happening in Veracruz. And Duarte resented this: "With security issues, you can do ninety-nine things right, but if one thing goes wrong, that's the story," he complained after the country found out that state police officers had disappeared four young people in their twenties and a teenager in the municipality of Tierra Blanca. They had been intercepted at a police check point after they celebrated a birthday party at the beach.[11]

The story in every media outlet should have been that the first four years of Duarte's administration saw 2,457 registered homicides. That's 12 per week, and that is just the official figure. Journalists have had to develop new ways of reporting, without getting injured or killed, on a grisly phenomenon that isn't new in Veracruz but the dimensions of which are now mind-boggling: the discovery of mass graves, since 2011, numbering in the hundreds. (As of April 2018, 30,000 human remains had been found, corresponding to an indeterminate number of people, in forty-four municipalities across the state. The Duarte administration is accused of covering up at least 1,824 missing-persons cases.)[12]

Around 2010, when Duarte became governor, there was a shift in power in the world of organized crime. Los Zetas went on the defensive in the face of a blood-soaked campaign from the so-called Cártel de Jalisco Nueva Generación (CJNG), known as "Las Chivas," for the Chivas de Guadalajara soccer team, also from Jalisco state. In 2011, a branch of the CJNG, the criminal syndicate known as Los Matazetas (the "Zeta killers"), launched a campaign of terror against Los Zeta that it was so extreme it was impossible for the authorities to ignore. No effective measures to counter it were implemented, and it led to an especially brutal display of violence. On September 21, attorneys general and presidents of federal justice tribunals from the state and across the country were to attend a national convention at the Grand Fiesta Americana Veracruz hotel in Boca del Río.

The day before, Los Matazetas dumped the bodies of thirty-five people they had killed, their corpses marked with the letter

Z, across the city's principal thoroughfare, Adolfo Ruiz Cortines, in front of the Plaza Las Américas mall—just a mile away from where the judicial convention would be held. The conference went ahead, but even as the attendees were grappling with the impact of the bloody message, fourteen more dead bodies were found scattered in the area. On top of this, Los Matazetas initiated a social media campaign spreading rumors of bloody confrontations in the surrounding areas that set off a wave of panic. Terrified parents rushed to schools to pull their children out of classes.

Other massacres followed: thirty people were killed in October, twenty-eight more in November, in addition to many other killings on a smaller scale. With the cooperation of state security forces, the CJNG established their hegemony in the central part of the state, from the port district to the interior of the country, through the urban areas of Córdoba and Orizaba, while gaining influence in Xalapa. Through killings, beatings and torture, and through bribes, they had police and public officials, as well as business owners and taxi drivers, under their control.

But the spectacular violence of the war against Los Zetas (some called them "those of the last letter" to avoid speaking their name aloud) was seriously damaging the Duarte administration's image and putting pressure on the federal government to do something about what was happening in Veracruz. It became increasingly necessary to push back against the perception of widespread, uncontainable chaos in the state. To minimize the impact of the Zetas-CJNG war, they avoided armed confrontations in busy shopping districts and heavily trafficked areas and then clamped down on the press, ensuring that any violence that persisted in rural and urban areas remained hidden from view. Media directors and reporters were faced with the age-old "silver or lead" dilemma: take the money, or take a bullet.

On April 2, 2013, came a bitterly ironic spectacle—at least for journalists working in the state. At the same Grand Fiesta Americana hotel where the judges and prosecutors had gathered when Los Matazetas had left their bloody message, Duarte was lauded by newspaper owners from across the country, led by Ángel Nakamura López of AMEX, information coordinator for the news agency of the Asociación Mexicana de Editores de Periódicos (AME; Mexican association of newspaper publishers). Duarte had been in office for a little over two years, and in that time nine reporters had been assassinated in Veracruz and three had disappeared in suspicious circumstances. But in a fawning ceremony, the AME presented him with an award for "the efforts Veracruz has made to guarantee the full exercise of freedom of expression," according to Julio Ernesto Bazán González, the organization's general manager. Duarte responded, "This means a great deal to Veracruz and to my government because it confirms that, in the defense and respect for freedom of expression, we are on the right course, and in protecting journalists we are responding quickly with concrete actions to a great challenge that we are overcoming together."[13]

Duarte, however, couldn't keep the persecution of journalists under his administration from the rest of the country, thanks indeed to the fearless reporting of the independent journalists themselves. And news quickly spread abroad, gaining the international spotlight on one occasion in the unlikely venue of a literary festival. In a photo he tweeted on October 4, 2014, Javier Duarte is seen warmly greeting the writer Salman Rushdie, who seems to respond in kind. A few days later, Rushdie clarified on Twitter that his attendance at the Hay Festival in Xalapa, an annual literary event that originated in Britain and is now held in several countries, in no way indicated his support for Duarte.[14] But Duarte's press office continued to exploit photos taken at the festival to the fullest, widely disseminating photos of him with other international figures who had attended the festival, including writers, celebrities, and the directors of the event.

When he came into office, Duarte had enthusiastically supported holding the festival in the capital of Veracruz annually, beginning in 2011. He used it as a platform for self-promotion, but responding to criticism, festival organizers said that "some of the most prominent defenders of freedom of expression on an international level, such as Carl Bernstein, Wole Soyinka, and Salman Rushdie" had "sent clear, emphatic messages condemning the persecution of journalists in Veracruz." This mattered little to Duarte, and he continued to sweep violence under the red carpet, playing the role of the sophisticated cosmopolitan with an avid appreciation for culture and the life of the intellect.

In light of this, sixteen journalists, including myself,[15] wrote in our open letter:

> We are not opposed to the Hay Festival; we are opposed to its use for political purposes in a state where journalism can cost you your life. We have spoken with editors, journalists, and writers who support our demand but are concerned about the potential closure of one of the few spaces that can nurture culture and debate. We have also spoken with the residents of Veracruz who

are sickened by the way the government is promoting itself through the festival, but who also do not want the festival to leave Veracruz. We have heard from the organizers of the International and Latin American Hay Festival, who approached us and offered to start a dialogue with journalists, writers, and editors to explore the situation.[16]

The petition was met with support by twenty-five Mexican and international organizations, and over three hundred journalists and writers from twenty-four countries signed it, including Jody Williams, Noam Chomsky, Javier Valdez, Artur Domosławski, Alma Guillermoprieto, Juan Villoro, Leonardo Padura, and María Teresa Ronderos. "A celebration of freedom and culture such as the Hay Festival cannot be held within a context of violence against freedom and culture," we concluded, because "it harms the memory of our assassinated colleagues."[17]

"The response to the massacre of [the workers of the French weekly] Charlie Hedbo was not to close the magazine, but to print 5 million copies. This is the model we identify with," responded Hay Festival director Peter Florence and international director Cristina Fuentes la Roche on February 6, 2015. "We believe in compromise, not in withdrawal; in the word, not in silence or emptiness." Notwithstanding, "we have heard the sentiments of a large part of the intellectual community," and as a result, instead of holding the festival "in a particular place, we will celebrate the festival on a digital platform, so as to reach not only our friends in Xalapa, but everyone who has access to the internet in Mexico."[18]

The following year, the Hay Festival in Mexico was relaunched in the city of Querétaro, in the state of the same name.

They resented Duarte at *Proceso,* the magazine, where Regina Martinez had worked as a correspondent. The staff there knew that the people who were actually responsible for the murder of Regina Martínez had not been caught. They knew that Duarte's prosecutors had tried to frame the homicide as the result of a misguided love affair, the fatal error of a single woman starved for love, who let herself be taken in by the first man who tried to seduce her. Duarte, for his part, knew their position and, in an attempt at damage control, went to the weekly magazine's offices to protest his innocence. Unsurprisingly, he was met with hostility. "We don't believe you," snapped *Proceso* director Rafael Rodríguez Castañeda, and the staff loudly rebuked Duarte as he left.

The following year, the journalist assigned by *Proceso* to cover Regina's case, Jorge Carrasco, broke a story, revealing even more flaws in the investigation into Regina's murder. The judge sentenced Jorge Antonio Hernández Silva, one of the alleged killers, even though there was absolutely no evidence, including fingerprints, that he had been present at the scene of the crime. The story immediately put Carrasco in danger. The magazine found out about a meeting between former and current officials from the state attorney general's office and the Secretariat of Public Security, in which they discussed what action to take against Carrasco. According to Carrasco, they decided to send police officers to Mexico City, where he was based, and kidnap the reporter and hurt him if he resisted. *Proceso* made it clear that they would hold the Veracruz state government responsible for any aggression committed against Carrasco and his family. The same went for Noé Zavaleta, who was their Veracruz correspondent, and all of the personnel who worked for the magazine.[19]

Zavaleta told me he had not met with any violence, but he has been the target of defamation campaigns that originated from the Veracruz state government and PRI party email accounts. He has been denounced as a gay drug addict in emails sent to business leaders, politicians, and directors and editors of media companies and newspapers, as well as to other journalists. The most dangerous were accusations that he was in league with one of the criminal syndicates battling for control of the state: aside from what the public might think, if a member of one of the criminal organizations seriously believed that Zavaleta was working for the enemy, there would be a price on his head.

Zavaleta was also aware that his movements were being closely monitored. The Duarte administration used the police and government employees to keep reporters under surveillance and generate as threatening an atmosphere as possible for reporters. Having at least one person watching you was par for the course when reporting in Xalapa. In April 2015, from Plaza Lerdo, or Plaza Regina, in front of the government palace, Rubén pointed out to my colleague Laurence Cuvillier up to fourteen "ears" who "monitor every demonstration, make audio recordings like they were interviewing us, but they don't ask questions, they just record information, and that is going on every day." The government's stalking of reporters is as intense as it is disorganized. There were so many, Rubén said, "they don't even recognize each other." It's not unusual for these "ears" to interfere with journalists' work, preventing them from taking photos. If they are taking pictures of reporters, the best response is to not object. After all, according to Rubén, "you could wake up dead."

"Aside from taking pictures of the demonstrators and the protest signs, they have to inform on what reporters were there, and from what media outlet," Zavaleta explained to me. "They are so obvious because they're very clumsy. They're not trained to do any kind of intelligence work. They make us nervous. They piss us off. Because there are ears from the General Directorate of Regional Politics [state government], from the Under Secretary of Government [state], ears from CISEN [federal intelligence], ears from the Secretary of Government [federal], ears from the Secretary of Public Security [state], police in plainclothes. At some events there are more ears than reporters."

Although Rubén was a *chilango*, a native of Mexico City, he had been able to create a real home for himself in Xalapa, with a strong circle of friends, including Nadia Vera. Nadia was a social anthropologist at the University of Veracruz and a social activist, She was a key member of the state's chapter of the #YoSoy132 movement, which had started during the 2012 presidential election, when students at the Universidad Iberoamericana, a leading private university, protested PRI candidate Enrique Peña Nieto during his visit, forcing him to hide in a bathroom. The movement demanding that politics be more democratic and more transparent quickly was taken up by university students across the country.

Rubén and Nadia met at a protest, and it was she who introduced him to Itzamná Ponce, a dancer from Pahuatlán, a town in the Northern Sierra of Puebla. In 2013, Nadia organized an event that included a performance in which Itzamná took part and which Rubén had photographed. Twenty-three years old at the time, Itzamná was beautiful, her fine features reflecting her native Nahua and European ancestry. She and Rubén soon they formed a little family along with Cosmos, a cocker spaniel.

Suppression of any open form of dissent was intensifying at the time, as the state and the country as a whole experienced increasing political turmoil in response to the relentless violence as well as the endemic corruption among those tasked with running the country. But while in Mexico City, students had more latitude to protest, in Veracruz, protestors were harassed and attacked. Nadia was no stranger to police brutality. On November 20, 2012, a demonstration was held at the annual parade marking the anniversary of the 1910 Revolution. Nadia Vera was pulled aside, harassed by some female police officers who stole her cell phone, put her in their car, and took her for a "ride" (drove her around while beating and threatening her), letting her out later on the street. Meanwhile, Rubén was told that some students who had hung a banner protesting the governor from a window of the Hotel México, in downtown Xalapa, were being beaten by plainclothes police officers. Rubén was spotted photographing the students as they were taken into custody. A man shoved him up against a wall and reminded him of the murder of the *Proceso* correspondent, which had happened six months earlier: "Better stop it if you don't want to end up like Regina!"

The following year, Rubén was ready for them: at dawn on September 14, 2013, riot police attacked an encampment of teachers protesting new education policies, in Plaza Lerdo. Secretary of Public Security Arturo Bermúdez had armed his officers with cattle prods. Rubén was chased by police, cornered in an alley, beaten, and forced to hand over his camera's memory card. But Rubén managed to dupe them. As he ran, he had managed to switch the memory card, concealing the one that had been in his camera and that contained the only images that would be published of the attack the next day in national media.

Rubén was fast becoming a headache for the state government. On February 16, 2014, the cover story of *Proceso* was a report by Zavaleta with the headline "Veracruz: lawless state." The image on the cover was a photo Rubén had taken of Duarte wearing a baseball cap and a white shirt with his name embroidered on it in red, his paunch spilling over his belt, the buttons on his shirt threatening to pop under his sweaty face. The following week, it was impossible to find a single copy of *Proceso* at any point of sale throughout Veracruz state: all of the copies had been bought up as soon as they arrived from Mexico City.

A few months later, the house where Nadia Vera lived was ransacked while she was out. "It had been such a total mess before that, for me to even notice they had been there, [the intruders] had to straighten things up and do a little cleaning," she told her friends. "That's the only reason I noticed. Later I saw that someone had even taken a shower."

She handled it with humor, but after telling her friends she could not bear the threatening atmosphere any longer, she decided not to wait around to see what would come next.

Nadia left for Mexico City in November 2014. A few days before she left, Nadia had done an on-camera interview with Rompeviento TV, in which she said, "They killed Regina Martínez and nothing happened. They just killed Gregorio Jiménez, another journalist, and nothing happened. We have how many journalists killed now and nothing's happened. Because criminal organizations govern this state. They are in charge. Los Zetas, literally, are running the whole state." Then Nadia said, "We hold Javier Duarte de Ochoa, the state governor, and his whole cabinet completely responsible for anything that might happen to us."[20]

2

Rubén Espinosa II

On June 30, 2015, in Poza Rica, a city in Veracruz known for its oil production, the governor invited journalists to a dinner to celebrate World Press Freedom Day. As always, attendants would receive gifts, tokens of appreciation for using their freedom to follow the official party line. This time, they would get a little something extra: a scolding and a warning.

"I'll say this for you, for your families," Duarte said, "but also for me and my family, because if anything happens to you, the one who gets crucified is me. Behave yourselves!"

There was nervous laughter among the journalists.

"We all know who's going down the wrong path," Duarte continued. "We're going to shake the tree and a lot of bad apples are going to fall. Don't confuse freedom of expression with representing the delinquents."

A few hours after the governor's speech, 140 miles to the south in Medellín, journalist Juan Mendoza Delgado, who had reported on organized crime and local politicians, was run over and killed in a hit-and-run accident. At least, that was what the official report said. Noé Zavaleta did not believe it for a minute: "A phantom car ran him over. They don't know who killed him. And a strange bandage was on his head. No one knows where that came from, since as we know there's no paramedic unit or Red Cross there. When the police found him, he was dead. The taxi he drove was never found."

Even though Juan managed the news website Escribiendo la Verdad (Writing the Truth), they claimed he was not a reporter but a taxi driver, and therefore his death had nothing to do with journalism. They categorized his death as just another accident that did not merit the resources necessary for a comprehensive investigation. To organizations defending freedom of expression, however, it brought the death toll of journalists assassinated under Duarte's administration up to thirteen.

A few weeks earlier, on June 5, a phone call had woken Rubén up very early in the morning. He woke Itzamná, who was sleeping beside him. "Something's happened," he told her. "I have to go!" A group of students from the University of Veracruz had been attacked on Calle Herón Pérez in downtown Xalapa, just two blocks from the state's PRI headquarters. Zavaleta and other reporters also rushed to the scene.

Eight student activists between the ages of nineteen and thirty-two, four of them women, had been celebrating a birthday. After midnight, around ten men burst in and "they were beaten up, not only with fists, but with baseball bats, sticks with nails in them, and machetes," Zavaleta said. "The room was covered in blood." The attack was executed by professionals who knew exactly the right amount of harm to inflict, causing no more nor less damage than they intended: none of the victims died, but they all suffered serious emotional trauma as well as permanent injuries, some with prominent, permanent scars on their faces, others brain damage.

A friend of several of the victims, Rubén called reporters together to organize a press conference and send a report to state media outlets and some in Mexico City. According to Rubén, the message behind the attack was "We can do whatever we want. We can enter your house and do whatever we want to you. And if we want to, we can kill you, and if we don't want to, we won't."

Over the course of the day, Rubén noticed several men staring at him pointedly and taking photos. Finally, near his home, two of them approached him. "They walked right at me. I stood with my back against the wall, and one of them passed by so close I could feel his breath. I stepped aside, I didn't look at him, I went on my way, then I turned around and they were staring at me. They were dressed in black."[1]

Rubén felt them closing, like a rough rope tightening around his neck. "I don't want to wind up like those guys," Rubén said to Itzamná. "I don't want to get hurt." And one day while eating tacos with some friends from a stand in Plaza Zaragoza, Rubén told them, "I'm leaving before they beat the shit out of me and drive me crazy, crazier than I already am." He planned to seek safety for a month or two in his hometown of Mexico City. Suspecting that his cell phone was tapped, Rubén called a friend to tell her he was leaving the next morning, but that was a ruse—he left two days later.

Rubén was not entirely convinced that Mexico City was safe, but he did not believe that exile meant he should have to hide in a corner and cry over his troubles in silence. "It makes me so angry and sad that a person can decide the course of my life, that he decided how or when I have to leave," he said in an interview on Rompeviento TV, speaking about Duarte.[2] In the capital, he couldn't cover the subjects he specialized in—social justice movements and their violent repression. The cost of living was too high, and he had to depend on his friends. He was far away from Itzamná. On the other hand, Xalapa meant risking death.

Rubén decided not to file any complaints or seek the protection of any government agencies "because I don't trust any state institution," even as he continued to work in support of activists in Xalapa to discredit the official story of the savage attack on the students' birthday celebrations of June 5. "We suspect elements of the Secretariat of Public Security covered for the attackers, or they themselves were the attackers," a group of Xalapa activists said in a statement Rubén sent out to the media, even though the police "insist they only showed up to help us, which is completely false." Once again, they believed, the police were complicit in attacks against activists. The statement warned that "we will present evidence of how they colluded with a group of individuals who intervened at the scene."[3]

Neither Juan Mendoza Delgado's killing nor Javier Duarte's speech at the World Press Freedom Day dinner could silence Rubén, even though he fully understood the governor's message: "It's an indirect threat against everyone who is not aligned," he told Zavaleta.

Ruben himself felt that he had a target on his back, although some of his friends thought he might be exaggerating. Nonetheless, he continued to denounce the Duarte administration in national and foreign media. "I just ask people, the public and journalists to turn around and look at Veracruz, because they are killing freedom of expression there," Rubén said to Shaila Rosagel, journalist for Sin Embargo.[4] He explained to Noemí Redondo of the Spanish agency Sin Filtros that under Duarteism, "They can break into your house and kill you and nobody will do anything, because they're afraid they'll get killed, too."

Still, Rubén began to worry that he might be overexposing himself: "Enough martyrs and heroes; we have to be human beings and understand there are some things you can't build in a day. We can be more effective alive than dead." He even felt he had opportunities in Mexico City, in spite of the limitations of exile: "I'm starting over, with a life I haven't adjusted to, but at the end of the day, it's a life, and looking at it very realistically, I'm lucky to be alive."[5] Less than a week later, he would be dead, his body shot execution-style along with four others, including Nadia Vera, in that apartment in Narvarte.

On August 2, 2015, at the base of the 171-foot column that supports the Angel of Independence in Mexico City, dozens of photographers wore masks of a black-and-white photo of Rubén's face and held up their cameras. The Angel, emblematic of Mexico City, is one of the most important symbols in the country. Soccer fans celebrate victories here and reporters come here to protest our dead. There were four hundred of us there that day protesting and brandishing posters that read "You can't kill the truth by killing journalists" and "Duarte's government + journalist assassins." One activist held up a Mexican flag on which the symbol at its center, an eagle devouring a snake, had been scrawled over in black ink with the message: "Honest journalist, dead journalist." We were not all journalists. People didn't just gather for Rubén.

A group of women came to mourn for the four women who had been murdered in Narvarte—the most recent victims of the tide of violence against women that was sweeping the country. Friends of Rubén and Nadia arrived from Xalapa, carrying with them feelings of grief, pain, and fear. Zavaleta sat down on the marble steps at the base of the monument and cried: "I don't know if it's even worth demanding justice. In the end I'm never going to see Rubén again."

Cameras, sunglasses, photos of the victims and photos taken by Rubén, and white carnations were laid atop a little makeshift altar on a heavy sheet of ochre paper. "Justice!" was written across the paper in yellow. "Not one more!"

After the last journalist was assassinated under the Duarte government—the eleventh—Rubén had gone out to protest, carrying a poster that read "I don't want to be number 12." Zavaleta said, "I still can't understand how Rubén became a statistic himself." He may not have been number twelve—twelfth was Juan Mendoza Delgado and thirteenth was Moisés Sánchez, but he was number fourteen.

"The entire field of journalism has been terrified by this crime," said Marcela Turati, a member of Red de Periodistas de a Pie. "This murder defied everything that he believed would protect him. The fact that he worked for important national media outlets counted for nothing, nor did it do any good for him to come to Mexico City, which was once considered a bubble where the violence from local governments wouldn't reach."[6]

"His horrible death, his torture, and Nadia's . . . haunt me," said journalist Pedro Canché. "They died for thinking, which seems to be banned in this country, since idiots are the ones who are rewarded. We would all do well to shake off the parasites. They are small in number, but how they plague us. They make the rest of us believe we are screwed."[7] In Mexico City, right in front of the scene of the crime in Colonia Narvarte, the Rexiste collective, a group of artists for social action, wrote in giant white letters in the street: "It was you, Duarte." Protesters took to the streets in the capital and in Veracruz, holding vigils demanding justice. On August 10, one thousand protesters marched from Plaza Lerdo to Casa Veracruz, the governor's official residence.

In smaller numbers, groups of journalists organized events throughout the month of August all over the country. Even in areas that have suffered the most violence, the murders committed in the heart of the nation had a powerful impact. In the state of Sinaloa, for example, where politicians work hand in hand with criminal organizations run by the likes of Joaquín "El Chapo" Guzmán, journalists held a little meeting in downtown Culiacán, where journalist Javier Valdez weighed in: "We have a corrupt government, incapable of bringing about conditions to live well in this country. If there aren't conditions to live, there aren't any to practice journalism. There is no right to freedom of expression."

Outrage extended beyond Mexico's borders. In Buenos Aires, sports photographers took advantage of the final game of the Copa Libertadores soccer championship to display the phrase, in a collective photo taken over the field, "No more genocide in Mexico."

"This is a watershed moment," read an open letter from five hundred journalists from across the globe on August 15. "[Mexico City] was one of the last safe havens in the country for reporters. Now there are none." Organized by PEN America and the Committee to Protect Journalists, the letter was sent to President Peña

Nieto, with signatures from high-profile people from forty countries, including Javier Valdez, Salman Rushdie, Margaret Atwood, Diego Luna, Noam Chomsky, Alfonso Cuarón, J.M. Coetzee, Guillermo del Toro, Paul Auster, Seymour Hersh, Alan Rusbridger, Gavin MacFadyen, Arianna Huffington, and Christiane Amanpour. The letter demanded that crimes against journalists be investigated and that freedom of expression be guaranteed: "Organized crime, corrupt government officials, and a justice system incapable of prosecuting criminals all contribute to reporters' extreme vulnerability."[8] The letter inspired the #NoNosCallarán (you won't shut us up) movement, in which seven hundred thousand people signed a petition demanding an independent investigation into the Narvarte murders.[9]

"The first thing we need to offer to guarantee justice for the victims is that there will be no impunity for those responsible. They will be dealt with, no matter who they are," declared Mexico City mayor Miguel Ángel Mancera, who ordered Mexico City's attorney general Rodolfo Ríos to act with diligence. But tragically, the authorities in Mexico City had no better intentions than their counterparts in Veracruz. That was clear in the way they continued to mislead the victims' families. There had been the incident when Rubén's sister Alma was told by police officers at the crime scene that a suspect had been arrested and that it could be her brother—both lies. Later that same day, at the attorney general's homicide department, an official recommended that Rubén's work as a journalist should go unsaid: "You can't say what his profession was because that could confuse the investigation." When Rubén's sister Patricia asked for his personal effects, first they told her that she couldn't have them "because they're soaked in blood and it's unsanitary and why would you want them?" Later, she was told, "The man didn't have anything, no wallet, no ID, no phone, and because of that he remains unidentified."

This was just the start. Seemingly at every turn, the authorities would throw impediments in the way of the family and their legal representatives as they sought justice for Rubén. Access to the investigation files was blocked, and they were given misleading information. The police clearly had no interest in solving the crime. They called in Ernesto Ledesma, the director of Rompeviento TV—where both Nadia and Rubén had declared Duarte responsible for anything that might happen to them—for questioning, and "the questions were not about the statements they had given us. They didn't ask anything about the governor or the harassment [Rubén and Nadia] experienced in Xalapa. The questions they asked me were: 'Do you know if Rubén Espinosa and Nadia Vera drank? Do you know if they smoked marijuana, if they partied?'" This was unacceptable to Ledesma: "Not only did they not protect them when they were alive, they didn't in death either. They're trying to destroy their reputations."

The strategy of attorney general Rodolfo Ríos and his second-in-command, Edmundo Garrido, was to stigmatize and criminalize the five victims, according to Leopoldo Maldonado, a lawyer with Article 19, which represented the Espinosa family. It was, he said, an elaborate exercise in character assassination. While the prosecutors and investigator didn't actually say it, they fed details to certain media outlets to suggest to the public that "partying, drug dealing, and prostitution" were what led to the murders.

Aside from Nadia and Rubén, the other victims were forty-year-old Alejandra Negrete, a domestic worker and mother of three who unfortunately had been there to clean the apartment that day (her body was the only one that exhibited no signs of violence other than a gunshot to the head), and two of Nadia's roommates: eighteen-year-old Yesenia Quiróz, originally from Mexicali, near California, and thirty-one-year-old Mile Virginia Martín, nicknamed "Nicole," who was from Bogotá, Colombia. The fact that Yesenia and Mile were young, attractive, and from outside Mexico City was exploited to suggest they sold sexual favors, or dealt drugs, and that the killers had been invited by one of them to enter the apartment, and that they were the real target of the attack. The others were collateral damage.

There was no evidence to support this hypothesis. Even so, the unsourced leaks were quickly picked up by media and columnists and used as headlines or in the lead: "Duarte not implicated in crude robbery,"[10] "Narvarte: Drug deal theory supported,"[11] (Ricardo Alemán); "Narvarte apartment also a brothel: Five people dead, collateral damage from unfortunate visit"[12] (Ciro Gómez Leyva); "Deplorable stench of prostitution and drugs"[13] (Carlos Marín).

This narrative was promoted most conspicuously by *La Razón*, a daily newspaper helmed at the time by Rubén Cortés. A tabloid that did not depend on subscription revenue, *La Razón* counted on the high impact of cover stories with sensational headlines, which assured it a prominent place on the newsstands. Its goal was not to inform but to shock. In this case, the paper claimed it was granted exclusive access to the attorney general's files from day one. It doubled down on the official interpretation of events, focusing increasingly on generating suspicion around Mile. She was the tabloids' easiest target. They published two photos of her aimed at heightening suspicions of illicit activity: in one, she is wearing a sexy black dress, posed next to a red and white Mustang she owned; in another she is wearing a blue bikini.

La Razón was relentless: "Narvarte victims knew their killers" (August 2); "Attorney general detains rapist who confessed: Yes, I was there" (August 5); "Killers brutalized Mile, the Colombian: Arrested" (August 6); "Rubén Espinosa found positive for marijuana and cocaine" (August 13); "Narvarte victim had multiple identities: Mile, Nicole" (August 17); "Purchases made by unemployed Mile investigated" (August 18); "Suspect arrested in Narvarte Case only went to apartment for sex" (August 19); "They went to the Narvarte apartment to settle a drug deal" (September 1); "We were only after Nicole, we didn't know the others" (September 2); "The Narvarte Killers went to kill Mile the day before but she wasn't there" (September 3).[14]

Ríos arrested three people in August and September—Daniel Pacheco, Abraham Tranquilino, and Omar Martínez—whom they described respectively as a street juggler, a parking valet, and an ex-convict, without explaining how these three were also experts in the use of firearms and torture techniques, as the evidence suggested. The authorities also presented very blurry fragments of security camera footage showing someone stealing the Mustang, which was later found abandoned nearby. According to *La Razón*, the official narrative was based on expert analysis and statements from the suspects that were part of the official investigation. The lawyers for the victims' families have countered those claims, asserting that they are all false. The official investigation then claimed that Mile's body had been the most battered of all the bodies found at the scene of the crime. This didn't match what Rubén's sister Alma and Yesenia's mother, Indira Alfaro, saw. They maintained that the bodies of Nadia and Rubén exhibited more brutal treatment than the others.[15]

Less than a week after the murders, seven prominent human rights organizations expressed their alarm that the attorney general's office was releasing isolated details in an apparent attempt to manipulate public opinion.[16] The Federal District Human Rights Commission, an independent public entity in Mexico City, lodged a complaint that the release of this information was violating the victims' fundamental rights, and a judge ruled in favor of the Espinosa family and ordered the attorney general to stop releasing information on the case.[17]

But the strategic leaks continued for three months until, in December, Ríos announced that a staffer had been detained. "I can't give you any details," he explained, because of the judicial order.[18] It had no effect on *La Razón*, which continued to publish its "scoops" into the new year: "Fingerprints, photos, videos, phone calls condemn Narvarte killers" (January 31, 2016); "With techniques from USA, Canada and Germany, the attorney general solved the case" (February 4).[19]

Meanwhile, according to the attorney general, the case had effectively been brought to a close—on November 27, 2015, barely four months after the crime. Edmundo Garrido, the prosecutor in charge of the case, sat down with the news site Animal Político to talk about the case. He said: "Three individuals took the lives of these five people who were inside, and these three individuals had a bond of friendship and affection with one of the people inside"—the Colombian woman, Mile Virginia Martín. But why would they have gone from being friends with a young woman to torturing and killing her and four people they didn't know?

The attorney general did not have "sufficient evidence to confirm the motive one hundred percent," Garrido admitted. He said, however, that the suspects in custody had confessed, and if there were any contradictions in their accounts, they were inconsequential. There was enough evidence to prove their involvement. He said they had committed the crime in three hours, entering the building at noon and leaving at three in the afternoon.[20] This ignored the fact that Rubén had sent a message on WhatsApp to his photographer friend at 2:13 p.m. Even if there were some truth to the official version of the story, the killers must have been hiding somewhere inside the building from noon until at least 2:14 and carried out the torture and execution of the five victims in silence—the neighbors did not hear anything—in just forty minutes, giving them six minutes to leave.

Although all five victims had been shot in the head, the attorney general said they could not establish who fired the gun, or how, nor did they ever recover a weapon. The statements allegedly obtained from the suspects served to give the impression that the motives were clear: Tranquilino said that Mile received shipments of cocaine at the Mexico City airport and that the three suspects had gone to steal a package of drugs from her, without any corresponding statement from the other two suspects or any confirming evidence; Pacheco said, "We went there to have sex, and after we had sex, Alejandra, the cleaning woman, asked me to leave and I waited for them outside." But examinations of the bodies showed that none of the four women had had sex, either consensually or not.

In any case, if Mile was the target of the attack, attorney Salas asked: Why were the others killed? Why were Nadia and Yesenia strangled? Why were Nadia and Rubén tortured?

Criticism of the attorney general of Mexico City—for not taking into account Nadia's and Rubén's work and activism in Veracruz and the harassment and threats they had received—was gaining traction, pushed by journalists and human rights defenders. The attorney general claimed such criticism was unjustified and asked to question Duarte, who quickly agreed to participate. But he demanded that all questions be submitted beforehand in writing and that the questioning take place in his offices in Xalapa. The attorney general agreed, and the questioning was carried out as Duarte wanted, on August 11. Representatives of the victims' families attended, but they were not allowed to ask any questions.

The questioners didn't make it hard for Duarte:

Question: Do you believe conditions in the state of Veracruz are currently suitable for carrying out journalistic activities?

Duarte: Yes.

Question: Has your government implemented any public policy that guarantees the human rights of journalists and reporters with respect to their work?

Duarte: Yes.

Question: What is your opinion of the photograph taken of you by Rubén Espinosa and published on the cover of issue number 1946 of *Proceso*?

Duarte: It's a good photo.

Question: Does Rubén Espinosa's work make you in any way uncomfortable in your role as governor?

Duarte: No.

Question: Do you believe the government of Veracruz respects the human rights of journalists and demonstrators?

Duarte: Yes.[21]

* * *

The back-and-forth continued in a similar vein. "I answered all of their questions and I made it clear that I am completely unconnected to the events," Duarte stated in a press release. He said that he did not believe in any law that protected the governor from legal proceedings, and so he agreed to testify, a move that he described as "an unprecedented event in the political and juridical history of Mexico." He also criticized "the public lynchings that, far from being credible, push away the truth and shield the real guilty parties." He closed the press release with, "The truth will set us free."[22]

Five other Veracruz state officials answered questions a week later, with the same results. Among them was Veracruz's secretary of public security, Arturo Bermúdez, whose arm reaches all the way to Mexico City—he is the owner of six armed personal security companies that operate in the nation's capital.[23] These businesses have offices in the neighborhoods of Independencia and San Simón Ticumac—both around a five- to ten-minute drive from the apartment where Nadia, Rubén, Alejandra, Mile, and Yesenia were killed.

The attorney general did not deem it necessary to investigate.

Nor did he make any effort to question people who knew

Rubén and Nadia. They did not call any reporters to testify about the risks of working in journalism under Duarte's government, to debunk the governor's assertion that conditions in his state allowed for freedom of expression, or to detail the aggressive harassment that forced Nadia and Rubén, like so many others, to leave Veracruz. What's more, the attorney general did not see any need to explain—if the three suspects they arrested were actually responsible for the crime—why they would have done it, what the motive was for torturing and then killing five people. Rubén's sister Patricia said to me, "They told us they are under no obligation to determine the motive; they simply have the three under arrest and they are not obligated to tell us anything more."

A year after the murders, attorney Karla Micheel Salas, who represented the families of Nadia and Mile, had still not been given any answers to the questions she had submitted to the attorney general.[24] Two years later, the Federal District Human Rights Commission released a report cataloging "errors and irregularities" in the official investigation.[25] Fingerprints, traces of DNA, and a shoe print were recovered by police investigators at the crime scene that corresponded to at least one other person who was not identified; evidence was missing or badly preserved (the commander of the homicide squad himself contaminated the crime scene by carelessly stepping on the blood-splattered floor);[26] the autopsies did not precisely determine the victims' cause of death or describe the injuries they sustained; the standard investigation protocols for femicides and for crimes against freedom of expression were ignored; and the numerous phone calls received and made by the accused were not investigated. What's more, by January 2016, Tranquilino and Pacheco had recanted their confessions. They said they had been obtained under torture.

On January 2, 2018, Article 19 Mexico released a report on the Narvarte case, calling it an "open wound." It found that, although the Human Rights Commission of the Federal District had released its own report to the Attorney General of Mexico City, they "had become merely an instrument of good intentions" and that no concrete action had been taken. No plans had been made to review the case or to follow up on other lines of investigation. The attorney general had gone so far as say, in front of the victims' families that there was nothing else to investigate, despite evidence presented to "strengthen the line of investigation related to the political persecution against Nadia and Rubén in Veracruz." That evidence was deemed irrelevant, and the attorney general's approach has been to relegate the case to oblivion.

"Three years after the crime," reads the report, "we as a society, and as family members of the victims, still do not know what happened. We do not know the motive for the crime, nor do we know with any certainty who the perpetrators were, nor its intellectual authors. Although the authorities make efforts to publicly present the case as closed, we insist that the Narvarte Case is and will continue to remain open until the right to the truth, justice, and a fair reparation is upheld, and until it is institutionally assured that crimes like this will not go unpunished."

Back in 2015, when Rubén and his colleagues launched Voz Alterna from a café in Xalapa, as they talked about the dire situation in Veracruz and what action they should take, he had made a comment that surprised and stayed with some of the people there. "I don't think they'd be so dumb as to come after one of us, but I have a feeling that one of us is going to be next." And they had come for him, taking his life in cold blood, along with four others. It was an enormous loss.

I strongly identify with Rubén. I admire his courage and honesty, the way he was so transparent. He was a great friend, as I would like to be, and I share his vision of journalism, his dissatisfaction with superficiality, apathy, and cynicism, as well as his passionate commitment to the public. "We're still here," he once said, "and we really believe we can do things well, that we can really manage the ethics involved in the right way. I believe there are very few of us, but we have great strength, because the truth is on our side."

3

Moisés Sánchez

At seven thirty in the evening on January 2, 2015, they came for her husband. The pickup trucks roared up to their home—a humble naked-brick two-storied construction—and screeched to a stop, letting out a group of men who approached the front door, yelling, "Where's the journalist?" María Ordóñez's two small grandsons, Axel and Jorge, had been playing out in the dirt road but upon seeing the men ran inside, frightened, where the boys' grandmother hugged them close. A few of the men stayed outside as lookouts. The others burst into the house, kicking down the door. They grabbed a laptop, a tablet, a camera, and two cell phones: the reporter's tools of the trade. Moisés Sánchez was fast asleep in the bedroom upstairs. After two long, exhausting days of work, the noise below didn't wake him. He woke when they hit him and dragged him out. María hugged the boys, hard: that was all that she could do. The boys watched as their grandfather was taken away.

A few months later, María was asleep in the bedroom she had shared with her husband. I was in the next room—a room of bare brick and cement walls and an iron grating for a window, no glass. It was three o'clock in the morning, but I couldn't sleep. The rains had swept in from the north to Medellín de Bravo on the out-skirts of Veracruz, a major port city on the Gulf Coast. The rain stayed outside, but the strong winds blew right in. The downpour pelted a large mango tree outside, shaking its leaves. It was the same mango tree under which Moisés liked to sit, relax, and read, to take refuge from the strong coastal sun. Now, two state police officers stood guard behind piles of sandbags ten yards away from the white front gate. At least they were supposed to be there—I could not make them out through the torrential rain.

Around twenty years earlier, Moisés's son, Jorge, used to climb that mango tree, and now his son's sons, seven-year-old Axel and eight-year-old Jorge, scrambled up its branches. They suffered what no one should ever experience, but what thousands of Mexican children and families are forced to endure: the violent abduction of a loved one right in front of their eyes.

That night I waited in darkness for the morning to come. Moi-sés hadn't had the chance to install electricity on the second floor. The scene of his abduction played over in my mind. I pictured the young boys, the men bursting in, Moisés dragged out, María help-less. A police car drove by in the night, its siren blaring, a sign of a protective presence. The night passed slowly.

In the morning, I went downstairs to the bathroom, which used water drawn from a hand-dug well. Looking into the living room through the thin curtain that hung in the doorway, I could see a television and two screens that showed video feeds from eight security cameras: five provided by the Federal Mechanism for the Protection of Human Rights Defenders and Journalists and three from the Veracruz State Commission for Attention and Protec-tion of Journalists. Barbed wired lined the exterior walls and fence. The murderers roamed free, while the family had to lock themselves up in their home.

Axel was in the living room by himself. He hadn't noticed me standing there. In fact, we hadn't yet met as he was already asleep when I arrived the night before.

"Hello, Axel," I said, gently pulling the curtain aside. He looked up. His gaze was wary, cautious, but not frightened.

"Who are you?"

"A friend of your dad's."

"Where did you just come from?"

"Upstairs, I spent the night upstairs."

He looked me over once more, then changed the subject: "Did you know some dinosaurs are made of water, and some are made of straw?"

I sat down to talk with him, and we chatted about this, that, and the other. I told him what I did for a living, but he didn't ask me anything about being a journalist—he already knew all about that, including the very worst.

October 2014 saw a wave of violence across the nation: there was, as I described before, the attack against Ayotzinapa students that left six killed and forty-three disappeared; also, a unit of soldiers killed twenty-two people in Tlatlaya, in Mexico State, at least fifteen of them after they had been detained; and two journalists were killed. In Mazatlán, a popular tourist destination on the Pacific coast in the state of Sinaloa, radio host Atilano Román was shot to death in his studio while on the air. In Ahome, another town in Sinaloa, the tortured body of the director of the magazine *Nueva Prensa*, Antonio Gamboa, was found.[1] Few paid attention because the killing of journalists had, tragically, become so commonplace.

The abduction of Moisés Sánchez the following January, six months before Rubén Espinosa's death, could have been lost in the tide of violence, but it stood out because it contained, however briefly, an element of hope. In Mexico, people joke about death but not disappearance. We know how to grieve, and the secular and the religious among us know how to open a path for our dead, to keep that emotional thread from breaking, pulling them back to us when we need them to advise us and comfort us, to listen to us, and talk to us, to eat and drink with us. But if someone disappears, if they are snatched away, there is nothing but anguish, the pain of not knowing, and within that a powerful hope that it might not be too late to see that person alive again. If they didn't kill him, if we don't have the body, there's a chance of saving him.

The police were slow to respond. It took them two hours to show up, despite the fact that witnesses said two agents were parked nearby as Moisés's abductors drove away. Since Moisés was relatively unknown, journalist groups were also slow to react. Someone on Twitter called for people to gather in front of the state of Veracruz representative's office in Mexico City, a French revival townhouse on Calle Marsella, to demand an immediate search effort for Moisés. The first hours after a disappearance are critical, and as the minutes tick by, the likelihood of finding the victim alive diminishes. Some of us who saw the tweet heeded the call. I got there first. The woman who tweeted showed up next. The two of us raised our signs in the air. Then other journalists showed up until we were twelve. As we protested, holding up our signs and chanting slogans, taking turns to be the demonstrators and the photographers.

Reporters in Xalapa and other cities held protests, drawing larger numbers. On January 8, the Voz Alterna collective called attention to the urgency of the situation in a session of the state congress. In a letter read aloud by Rubén Espinosa, they demanded that the investigation be conducted on the federal level, and not by the local attorney general's office, because that would essentially mean the kidnapping suspects would be in charge of the investigation.

But the authorities in Veracruz saw things differently. "He's not a journalist, he's a taxi driver," Governor Javier Duarte said.[2] To him, Moisés was not worth anyone's time. But public pressure grew. Their top priority was to quiet things down, discounting his work as a journalist, as if Moisés's job driving a taxi excluded any other work, according to Leopoldo Maldonado, an attorney representing Moisés's family and Mexico's legal officer for Article 19, a nonprofit advocacy group defending freedom of expression. "Their primary concern was not finding out where he was; they weren't worried about finding him alive."

In the case of Moisés, that hope was all too brief. His body was found on January 24, after three excruciating weeks of searching—three weeks spent fiercely clinging to hope in spite of the evidence pointing to the contrary.[3] It would be several more days before his son Jorge could be sure it was actually his father and not the body of a stranger presented to close the case, as had happened frequently before. The funeral was held on February 6, in Moisés's home, the house he had built with his own hands. On top of the gray metal casket rested a Minolta camera, a Sony video camera, and two photographs of Moisés. In those first weeks of uncertainty, Jorge had told his boys their grandfather would be home soon, that he was just out working, driving his taxi. But his death could not be hidden from the boys any longer. Or how they killed him.

"Let me see him," said Axel. "Let me see."

"Just wait a while, he's sleeping."

"But my friends say they cut him into pieces."

They abducted Moisés, beheaded him, dismembered him, and disposed of the pieces in black trash bags, which they threw by the side of a road. One person was arrested for the murder, a former police officer named Clemente Noé Rodríguez, who explained the motivation behind the sadism in a videotaped statement to the police: "He rocked the boat, they told us, but at first we didn't know he was a reporter, we thought he was just a taxi driver. But two days later we saw it in the news, and he published things that were damaging to city hall."[4]

Moisés's weapon had been *La Unión* . . . , of which he was the director, the sole reporter, the publicist, and the distributor. It was a simple black-and-white publication 8¼ inches high, 5½ inches wide, a standard letter-sized page folded in two. Moisés copied the originals on a photocopier and folded the pages himself. He produced about a thousand copies every month, or every few months, at a cost of twenty centavos per page, and distributed them for free to as many of the residents as he could reach. "At one point he tried to get advertising," but "not very many people were interested," Jorge remembers. "He only got two or three ads, but it didn't cover the cost. His goal wasn't to make money, but to inform."

For almost twenty years, Moisés worked like a traditional artisan: cutting out pictures and columns with scissors and using a glue stick to fix them to sheets of paper to be photocopied. A business card could become a newspaper ad. The masthead from the August 3, 1998, edition looks like it was handwritten in pen, with a little drawing depicting several stick-figure people climbing some stairs, and the heading "La Unión . . . weekly. Our motto: the truth above all, even if it hurts." For later editions, he used typeface to print a more ambitious tag line: "Informative media LA UNIÓN . . . The voice of Medellín." Recently, Jorge had learned how to lay out and design publications on a computer. With those skills, he helped his father give his newspaper a more modern look.

To make his living, Moisés undertook many jobs: he sold fresh produce, he was a butcher, he collected and sold scraps, he drove a taxi. This helped him to eke out a living: a passionate, self-taught reporter, Moisés left us revealing glimpses of who he was. For example, he recorded himself standing next to an old refrigerator, with a sheet of corrugated metal serving as a backdrop, delivering a promotional message for his newspaper. Of medium height, olive skinned, with a faint mustache and black hair just beginning to show some flecks of grey, he tries to ad-lib a sales pitch with not altogether successful results: "What's happening in Medellín . . . the news you want to see, right here." He pauses, trying to call to mind something specific to mention. He takes a deep breath. "News of weddings in the municipality . . . the news." A slight smile plays across his face. He looks amused by his own mental block. "The news about . . . sports." He grins and decides to cut the experiment short.

In his reporting, Moisés covered a wide range of subjects. He conceived of *La Unión* . . . as a community paper, covering everything from everyday goings-on in the municipal government to events at local churches, sports events, and festivals. But if that were all, a succession of mayors and governors would not have seen Moisés as a threat.

Moisés wrote open letters to authorities to remind them of the things they were not doing, where they were falling short, and the promises they had not kept. He covered washed-out roads, unfinished construction projects, and abuses of authority. In the beginning, he stayed away from reporting violent crime, because he didn't want to antagonize criminal organizations that were operating in the area, but the increasing number of bodies left by gang feuds became too high to ignore. So he started writing about them, too: the assaults, kidnappings, and murders, even writing about the municipal police who, just to make money, took local residents to a secret jail, where they were tortured until their families paid a ransom. That story did not appear anywhere in official records, to protect unspoken pacts of impunity. In 2014, the Executive Secretary of the National System of Public Security registered zero kidnappings in Medellin,[5] but during their investigation into Moisés's death, the state attorney general's office confirmed there had been eleven kidnappings that year.

Jorge told me his father used to say, "We have a government that came to power not to work, not to build a better town, a better Medellín. They have come to sack, to rob, to hand out jobs to their brothers, their brothers-in-law, their sons-in-law, to donors." Omar Cruz, the mayor of Medellín, felt at risk of being exposed by Moisés, who regularly reported on his administration's faults and how they contributed to the area's insecurity. The journalist told his son that Cruz had offered to pay him off periodically in exchange for supporting him in *La Unión*. But Moisés the journalist responded, "You can't possibly be saying you want to give me thirty thousand pesos a month to say nice things about you, while you can't even fix a broken streetlight or put in a sidewalk or pave the roads."

In Medellín de Bravo, the powers that be are fond of secrecy. They like to take care of things far from the prying gaze of outsiders. The region's principal economic activity is concentrated in the port city of Veracruz, which gives its name to this elongated state that hugs the coast of the Gulf of Mexico, and Boca del Río, a smaller port city just a few miles to the south. Next-door Medellín serves as a bedroom community for both cities. Tax revenue, or whatever remains after corruption has its way, tends to remain in the port cities, neglecting Medellín, where the workers live.

Nonetheless, Medellín, once a small country town, has grown in size with the prosperity of the nearby ports, but without any planning or control, it has taken on a character that's neither urban nor rural. There is a small administrative center, with a Town Hall, a building constructed in the 1970s, facing a simple church built in 1524 by Spanish captain Hernán Cortés, the second church erected in all of mainland America. Only about 3,000 of the municipality's 75,000 residents live in central Medellín. The rest are spread around the town, the poor in communities with next to no public services, and the middle class, who can't afford the higher prices along the coast, in housing developments.

Local production is dying out. Medellín had once been the state's leading mango producer, but the crop is no longer profitable, and landowners would now rather do business with real estate developers. Across the street from Moisés's house, there is a large tract of land—now shabby and rundown—where tons of fruit were harvested years ago. The land has been leased to a school.

Typical Medellín residents have moved from elsewhere, attracted by the low cost of living in the area's wetlands. Moisés and María moved there from the city of Veracruz in 1989, when their son, Jorge, was just four years old; they took up residence on a piece of land whose ownership was under legal dispute, along with around a hundred other people, living in houses made of wood, tin, and plastic. Eventually, they were relocated along with 350 other families to the El Tejar neighborhood.

Twenty years later, the area is still extremely impoverished. Dirt roads get washed out with the rain; garbage piles high. A water and drainage system is only now under construction. The one system that is up and running is a very basic public security system, and that is just as dangerous as the criminal networks.

Aside from writing about what was going on in *La Unión*, Moisés tried to let the public across the whole state of Veracruz know about the issues in Medellín, acting as a source for journalists at established local media (though the town has never made it to the national public eye: when Mexicans hear of Medellín, most think of the Colombian city). Moisés would seek them out and give them the latest news. He was the only source of information from Medellín. He told the stories that were supposed to remain untold.

Journalists in Xalapa were shaken by the attacks directed at them, which seemed to only increase in frequency and violence, while no one seemed to care. A tragedy that took place on the other side of the ocean only heightened that impression. Moisés was kidnapped on January 2. Five days later, in Paris, two terrorists stormed into the offices of the satirical weekly magazine Charlie Hebdo, killed twelve people, and injured eleven more. It was a carefully planned massacre, executed in cold blood, in retribution for some cartoons the magazine had published. Reacting to the attack on journalists in Paris, the public in Europe and other regions around the world erupted in shock and anger, pulling together in solidarity. Just as in other parts of the world, thousands of Mexican internet users added the hashtag #JeSuisCharlie to their social media profiles, and it appeared on signs at all kinds of demonstrations—including daily protests demanding the return of Moisés, alive. But few seemed to notice the misfortune that had engulfed the state of Veracruz. "In France everyone, and in Mexico no one . . . " Rubén posted on Facebook. "The difference is growing accustomed to [the violence] and distant continents, thoughts, logic, reasons and actions."

Acting in solidarity, journalist colleagues saved Moisés's newspaper. Reporters and photographers volunteered their services, and a new issue was printed with the support of Article 19. On February 12, 2015, just six days after burying his father, Jorge published the latest issue of *La Unión*. . . . It was officially unveiled in the offices of CENCOS (National Center of Social Communication)[6] in Mexico City, in a tabloid format, with a production quality that would have made its founder proud.

At the event, well-known journalist Javier Solórzano told Jorge: "Moisés's struggle is the never-ending struggle that you are taking up as his heir." Before his father was abducted, twenty-nine-year-old Jorge had been a graphic designer for a lifestyle magazine, *GB*.

Weeks after his father's body was found, he took over the citizen watchdog paper that had cost his father his life. "You know how to be a good son," Solórzano said. "You could have pursued something else, but now the path is leading you. I wanted to acknowledge that you didn't cower in a corner after suddenly losing your father. You emerged, holding your head high."

Jorge took the floor. Unused to speaking in public, he kept his eyes down, uncomfortable with being the center of attention. "I'm sure that all that time, no matter how terrible an experience he might have lived through, he never regretted what he did," he said. "It never would have crossed his mind to say, 'If only I had kept quiet, maybe I wouldn't be in this situation.'" Jorge said they produced this latest edition of the paper "so that Moises's philosophy, his hard work, everything he did would not be in vain. If we didn't do this, they would have won—the ones who ordered him silenced, the ones he made uncomfortable, the ones who gave the order to cut off a critical voice. *La Unión* . . . must stay alive because this must not happen again. We don't want to hear that another Moisés has disappeared anywhere else in Mexico. We don't want to hear another Moisés has been killed. *La Unión* . . . will go on, it will still be distributed, because it's our form of protest, our way of saying we are not afraid, we will not be silenced."

In February 2015, five months before his own death, Rubén Espinosa used his camera to document Jorge, walking through the picturesque streets of downtown Xalapa with reporter Arantxa Arcos and photographer Raziel Roldán, handing out free copies of the new issue of *La Unión*. . . . It read "Moisés's Medellín" on the front page and "Forced Silence" on the back cover. They offered the paper to people who asked for it and to the riot police who refused to take it. Some people backed away from them, afraid: in Veracruz, anything to do with the victims of crime could turn you into a victim yourself.

April 28, 2015, marked exactly three years since Regina Martínez had been killed, and no progress had been made in the criminal investigation. Jorge, Aranxta, and Raziel gathered with around two hundred activists and people who worked in the media in front of the government palace, a grand neoclassical building erected in 1855, where Duarte's office was located. Jorge led the way, megaphone in hand. One of the banners with Moises's portrait read "No more violence in Veracruz." "Regina lives!" shouted a young man in a white T-shirt, with a longish beard and a shaven upper lip. "The fight goes on!" Jorge and the crowd answered. "Moisés lives!" "The fight goes on!"

Only five more days would have to pass before the twelfth journalist to lose their life during Duarte's term was slain. On May 2, 2015, Armando Saldaña disappeared. His body was found two days later in the state of Oaxaca, six miles from the state line with Veracruz, with four bullets in it and signs of torture. Armando was from Veracruz, he worked for media outlets in Veracruz, he practiced journalism in Veracruz. But the Veracruz state attorney general didn't even try to investigate. To state attorney general Luis Ángel Bravo, the matter was very simple: if the body didn't turn up in Veracruz, it had nothing to do with him. "This discovery, unfortunately, was made in Oaxaca," he said to the press, "and I do not see any reason to investigate, since there is absolutely no evidence, no indication that would lead one to believe that something was committed here that would have had any impact on the discovery of Armando Saldaña. These are events that took place in Oaxaca and they are completely removed from the state of Veracruz."[7]

Journalists and other media professionals protested, not really expecting to be heard. Why would they, since discounting violence and disparaging the work of journalists were Duarte's stock-in-trade? In October, during a visit to the World Trade Center in Boca del Río, Duarte boasted, "I'm responsible for economic growth and the progress we've made in terms of security," since in Veracruz "they used to talk about shootings, murders, organized crime, and now we're only talking about shoplifting, somebody stealing a Frutsi [sugary drink] and some Pingüinos [cookies] from an Oxxo [convenience store chain]."[8]

El Sabueso (the sleuth), a fact-checking project that is part of the website Animal Político, said Duarte's assertion was "ridiculous." In 2014 in Veracruz state, two thousand businesses were robbed, five thousand vehicles were stolen, and three thousand residences were broken into and robbed: "To put it in the governor's terms, in Veracruz more cars are stolen than Frutsis and Pingüinos." What's more, according to Animal Político, 512 murders were committed in Veracruz in 2014. By October 2014, Veracruz ranked third in states with the most kidnappings, with 142 so far that year, an increase of 42 percent over the previous year.[9]

For the protesters gathered in front of Duarte's office on April 28, 2015, for Jorge, Aranxta, and Raziel, the "award" presented by publishers to recognize the Governor's efforts "to guarantee the full exercise of freedom of expression" was another source of outrage: "There they are, there they are, the truth killers!" they shouted. Jorge held up a black poster, with the map of Veracruz state outlined in red and "Attorney general of IMPUNITY" written in white letters. Behind him, a young woman held up a white sign that read: "We don't believe you." The crowd held up large pictures of Regina and Moisés.

"We don't believe them, and we let them know it," *Proceso* magazine had declared in an editorial about Regina's murder investigation. That phrase was taken up as a slogan at the protest. The little plaza in front of the government palace carries the name Sebastián Lerdo de Tejada, honoring a nineteenth-century president. "Since justice has not been served, we want to keep Regina's memory alive and today we rename this plaza, formerly called Plaza Lerdo, as Plaza Regina," journalist Norma Trujillo declared. Rubén Espinosa held the metal plaque inscribed with Regina's name and put it in place. The plaque was removed almost immediately, but Voz Alterna later returned with another one, this time fixing it to the ground with cement so it would be harder to remove.

Jorge did not visit cemeteries very often. He had only been to his father's grave three times in the few weeks after his father's death: first to make preparations for the funeral, then for the burial, and a third time with his son Axel. On the morning of April 30, 2015, he returned simply because he had a feeling he had to go there. Standing facing the grave, he recalled how he, along with family, friends, and neighbors, as well as public officials and the police, had warned Moisés that he was in serious danger, that his work carried too many risks, that he was making a huge sacrifice for people who did not fully appreciate it.

Jorge, and others, reproached Moisés for being blind to his family's anxiety. But his work came first in spite of the clear dangers.

Known as Moi by friends and foes alike, he said the only way to get the authorities to do something was by calling them out, showing what they had done. To Moisés, protesting was a way of life, a way of bringing about change.

In January of 2013, Jorge's wife, Adelina Tome (who was twenty years old at the time), had been hit by a bus that ran a red light. The driver had stopped and decided to put the bus in reverse to run over her again because "according to local law," Jorge explained, "it's cheaper to kill somebody than to injure somebody." If she survived, the driver would have to pay her medical bills and a fine. "People who were nearby saved me," Adelina remembered, "and kept the driver from running over me again. He wanted to kill me, but thank God they saved me."

Aside from the emotional and physical toll, there was the financial cost: within fifteen days, the family had spent around 80,000 pesos, approximately $6,000, in medical care, which the bus company refused to cover. Moisés and his family launched a publicity campaign that forced the authorities to get involved, but the owner of the company was an influential man who simply ignored court orders. After fighting for a year, they reached an agreement: the family accepted a payment of 90,000 pesos, which they badly needed to cover some of the 150,000 pesos they owed in unpaid medical bills.

Moisés was not a man who gave up, nor was he man who would let himself be bought. The authorities did not know what to do with him. The decision to have him killed may have been made in late 2014, when Moisés uploaded a video to YouTube that went viral throughout the state and was deeply embarrassing to the powers that be.

Moisés uploaded the video nineteen days before his abduction. Although the twenty-nine-year-old mayor of Medellín, Omar Cruz, was a member of the PAN (associated with blue), he was aligned with the PRI governor Duarte (associated with red) and known as a *panista rojo*. Ever since Cruz took office in December 2013, Moisés had pressed him to ask the Navy to take over security in Medellín—as had been done in other municipalities—and to dismiss the municipal police force, which was suspected of having close ties to organized crime. Cruz promised to do so, but the only naval officers that locals ever saw were the mayor's own security detail. The night before Moises uploaded the video, two of his neighbors had been wounded in gunfire, the latest in a long series of violent incidents that had claimed many lives, including that of a baby who had been senselessly killed during a home invasion. Residents of the El Tejar neighborhood had had enough; they decided to form their own self-defense committee.

The video takes place at night beside a street sign that reads "Tulipanes," the only light coming from the video camera. Moisés did not film anyone's faces; instead, he focused on the hands of a dozen local residents grasping machetes, who explained what they were doing: "Since the authorities won't come to our help, we're going to take justice into our own hands. We've suffered enough abuse," a woman says. A man continues, "They are warned, all the criminals, they have no reason to come into our neighborhood." One more offers his opinion of Mayor Cruz: "He has people in the Army watching his back. He doesn't even trust the police. So how are we supposed to trust the police?"

The video made waves in city hall and the state capital. According to Jorge, Moisés knew that Cruz had been berated by Duarte in a recent private meeting in Xalapa. Someone who had been in the meeting told Moisés about it. Duarte had said to Cruz, "How is it possible that you haven't been able to silence Moisés yet, that you haven't bought him?" Cruz had responded, "It's just that you can't talk to Moisés. He can't be bought. You're not going to get anywhere with money."

Most crimes in Veracruz are filed without being investigated; in this case, the state attorney general Luis Ángel Bravo held a press conference to give reporters their official version of the crime. Local reporters did not think this was done out of any sense of responsibility but because Jorge Sánchez had had the opportunity on February 6 to offer his criticism in an interview with Carmen Aristegui, the most popular news anchor on national radio, which ended up pressuring state authorities to show they were actually working on the case.

According to Bravo, the order to kill Moisés had been issued by Mayor Cruz and delivered by his driver, Martín López, to Clemente Noé Rodríguez and five others, known only by their aliases: "El Harry," "El Chelo," "El Piolín," "El Moi," and "El Olmos." The prosecutors' conclusions are based solely on Rodriguez's videotaped confession, which was uploaded to YouTube. In Mexico, in the absence of a firm case, statements like these are frequently fabricated by authorities and filtered out to the public to shape opinion in favor of the official version of what transpired. No one else has been arrested: not the driver, not the other alleged killers, and not the former mayor Cruz, who has since fled, his whereabouts still unknown. Jorge believes that Cruz was involved, but he assured me that people even higher up are being protected, people such as Governor Duarte.

The report produced by the State Commission for Attention and Protection of Journalists details five serious omissions in the official investigation into the murder, including "the absence of a line of investigation into what Governor Javier Duarte de Ochoa may have said about the journalist Moisés Sánchez Cerezo, before his disappearance," since that could have pointed to "some kind of reprisal" against the journalist.[10]

In March 2018, the two police agents who were parked by Moisés's house when he was abducted were convicted for neglect. Their sentence of twenty-five years in prison suggested that justice had been served, even though the case was far from solved. "They are not the ones who kidnapped my father," Jorge told the daily *La Jornada Veracruz*. "They aren't the intellectual authors. They're the ones who didn't respond to our call."

Death threats are hard to deal with. If you take them too seriously, you're handing victory to the ones making threats; but if you dismiss them, they may take your life. Moisés did not take them seriously. According to Jorge, his father said, "They can't be so stupid as to go after somebody with such a small newspaper, because that would just make it big."

Moisés Sánchez was a lone hero, but he wasn't a tragic figure. He was determined to overcome fear. He would say that "if things are how they are, it's because so many people have been afraid," Jorge explained. "He was an optimist, but he didn't just talk, he was an optimist who took action."

With its dark brown mosaic tiles, the tomb of Moisés Sánchez stands out from all the pale tombstones around it. The epitaph includes three of Moisés's mottos:

Everyone should do their part.

Living in fear is not an option.

Publishing the truth is for the brave.

His beliefs live on in Jorge: "If they thought by killing him they would win silence, they'll see that's not how it is—we're going to show them. It's my turn. It's my turn to demand justice and do what I have to do."

Trouble lay ahead for Duarte, and it seems only fitting that this chapter on Moisés end with the governor's downfall. On August 11, 2016, Noé Zavaleta, the journalist who had replaced Regina Martínez as *Proceso*'s Veracruz correspondent, had a launch event for his first book, *El Infierno de Javier Duarte* (Javier Duarte's hell), in Mexico City. The cover featured the unflattering photo Rubén Espinosa had taken that had so enraged the governor. Duarte was in the harrowing last days of his tumultuous term: The PRI had suffered stunning election defeats in seven out of twelve states a few months earlier, including Veracruz. Several journalistic investigations had exposed Duarte's involvement in huge fraud cases. Arturo Ángel and Víctor Hugo Arteaga of the news site Animal Político, with the support of the think tank Mexicans Against Corruption and Impunity (MCCI), documented a vast network of sham companies that Duarte used to embezzle 645 million pesos ($43 million) from the state budget. Worse still, he was being scrutinized not only by the press, but by rulers of their own party. In his 2012 presidential campaign, Enrique Peña Nieto had considered him one of the role models for the revamped PRI. But now, battered by one scandal after another, his administration needed scapegoats to ease pressure from the public. Peña Nieto said he would no longer have a hand in protecting them.

The opposition party was due to take power in Veracruz in December 2016. Even so Zavaleta did not want to tempt fate by launching his book in Veracruz. He had experienced some uncomfortable encounters with Duarte in the past. Back in 2014, they had met, at the governor's request, at the home of a mutual friend in El Estero, a residential neighborhood in the municipality of Alvarado, near the city of Veracruz. He was very friendly, almost tender, with the journalist, and after talking about the cover of *Proceso* with the photo taken by Rubén Espinosa, he wanted to know what Zavaleta needed so the magazine would "give him some breathing room."

"Look, Noé, I want to be your friend, we could be friends, tell me what you need," he offered, even as Zavaleta was being attacked by an email smear campaign. Zavaleta replied, "I told him, 'Yes, I do want something: I want to be left alone, just let me do my work.' His face fell. He was hoping I'd tell him give me a million pesos or buy me a house and that would be the end of it."

Soon after that, Mayor Cruz would tell him he had been unable to buy off Moisés Sánchez, either. Duarte faced a problem he did not know how to solve: reporters who could not be bought. In Mexican politics, there's an expression, "La moral es un árbol que da moras," popularized in the mid-twentieth century and attributed to PRI party boss Gonzalo N. Santos. Loosely translated, it means there are no ethics, only interests, and if Zavaleta did not accept a financial offer, it could only be because a rival had gotten to him first. Zavaleta had to explain to him that the critical coverage in *Proceso* was the magazine's mission, not a way to apply pressure in order to get some kind of benefit.

That is why, when it came to launching his book, Zavaleta went to Mexico City and decided to stay there for a while. At the event itself, at the Octavio Paz bookstore, the director of *Proceso* lamented that since the nation's capital was no longer a safe haven for journalists, Zavaleta had to be protected by bodyguards.

Meanwhile, Veracruz continued to sink into an abyss of violence and political dysfunction. Several more journalists were assassinated that year—including Pedro Tamayo and Anabel Flores. Duarte took a leave of absence from the governorship of Veracruz on October 15, 2016, just six weeks before the end of his six-year term. A judge had issued an order for his arrest on charges of corruption, money laundering, and involvement with organized crime. For once, in a country where the justice system routinely ignores journalistic revelations, an investigative report—in this case, the report by Arturo Ángel and Víctor Hugo Arteaga on the governor's morass of corruption–had been the basis for opening criminal proceedings. But it was more than could be expected that Duarte would be immediately placed behind bars. He escaped in a helicopter provided by interim governor Flavio Ríos. He was eventually detained in Guatemala in April 2017 and extradited to Mexico.

Despite the number of crimes laid at his feet, he was not held accountable for the deaths and disappearances of journalists under his governorship. I remember, shortly after his flight, at the federal Congress of the Union, opposition deputy and journalist Virgilio Caballero provided the very rare opportunity for a debate in a public forum with Ricardo Nájera, head of the Office of the

Special Prosecutor for Crimes Against Freedom of Expression: an office whose impressive name was inversely proportional to its efficacy. Created to streamline the judicial processing of crimes committed against journalists, it boasted a dubious record of winning just two convictions out of 798 cases it handled between July 2010 and August 2016. And over the two years that followed, since Nájera took the helm, they had only taken 40 cases: their real job was to distract.

I attended the debate, and when it was my turn to speak, I pointed out that Javier Duarte had escaped without the attorney general opening a single investigation into his possible responsibility in the killings and forced disappearances of twenty journalists, which all took place during his term as governor of Veracruz. With the facts in hand, I pointed out that instead of acting to help journalists, the office had become an obstacle, working to justify the actions of the authorities and not to help the victims of those actions.

"The information does not match the reality": Nájera dismissed the data and arguments, and offered an outrageous proposal in reply: "I think every journalist is an expert investigator. The Public Ministry is expert in investigation. Why not combine the expertise of each to perform a more direct investigation? We will work together, journalists and authorities."

At the end, he offered to meet with me in his office to explain in private what he could not explain in public. He did not say why. The event was over. Before leaving, I approached him and said, "I accept your invitation. But we are not interested in courtesy visits. Give me an on-camera interview." He had no reply. All he did was laugh.

4

Pedro Canché

Pedro Canché and Jorge Sánchez pose together for the camera. Rubén Espinosa is taking the photograph, unwilling to appear in it himself, but after attempts to persuade him, he gives in. The result is a photograph in which Pedro and Rubén, both smiling, stand on either side of Jorge, who has a serious look on his face, as though he is arbitrating a dispute. It is June 16, 2015, and the three of them have met in a restaurant in Mexico City's Roma neighborhood. Pedro Canché is a Mayan reporter from Quintana Roo who has been hiding out in Mexico City for just over two weeks; Jorge Sánchez is in the capital to meet with the Special Prosecutor for Crimes Against Freedom of Expression; and Rubén has arrived from Veracruz only a few days before. Also with them are Nadia Vera, who had fled Veracruz five months earlier; another Veracruz activist, Julián Ramírez; and the photographer who would regularly check in with Rubén for his safety and who would be the last known person to communicate with Ruben before his death.

The group talks about the governors of their respective states—Duarte in Veracruz and Roberto Borge in Quintana Roo—and find more than a passing similarity. Nadia is still shaken by her experiences in Veracruz; she is trembling. "Look, I have goosebumps," she says, showing Pedro her arm. Pedro talks about the corrupt governor of Quintana Roo, who is, as Rubén puts it, "like Duarte's twin brother." They are both arrogant and violent, and they hate journalists. "Do you think Duarte collects dead journalists?" Pedro asks. Rubén does not see him as a collector. He is "a criminal protected by president Peña Nieto, who should have pushed him out by now but instead tolerates his stance against journalists," Rubén says. "More than just pushing him out, he needs to be prosecuted. But they're part of the same criminal network, so that would be a stretch."

It is after midnight, and the restaurant is about to close. Pedro invites his friends to come to a protected house where the free speech organization Article 19 is hosting him, a nice place with a little kitchenette. There, they continue talking long into the night.

At some point over the course of one balmy Caribbean night, months earlier, the wooden looms in the prison had been repurposed as lethal weapons. During the day the prisoners used them to weave thick threads into brightly colored hammocks with the deft precision that only comes from long experience—they were the prisoners' sole source of income. That night, however, the inmates of Cellblock 2 at the city jail of Carrillo Puerto, Quintana Roo, prepared to defend themselves. The first order of business was to break down the wooden frames and sharpen the lengths of wood. They had been given a tip: the inmates of Cellblock 1, the maximum-security unit that held prisoners convicted for murder, kidnapping, or rape, would be coming for them, armed with guns and lead pipes. What Cellblock 1 didn't know was that Cellblock 2 would be waiting, ready for battle.

The target of the planned attack was Pedro, who had been imprisoned under false charges as payback for having humiliated Governor Roberto Borge's pride. To make an example of him, Borge had ordered the journalist to be locked up for twenty years. He might be willing to reduce his time if he showed sufficient contrition as well as evidence that he would fall in line and offer total submission to the governor. But Pedro did just the opposite. He made even more noise, gaining the support of human rights defenders and others who were sympathetic to his plight. From behind bars, he systematically denounced the abysmal conditions there, writing letters in pencil and smuggling them out of the prison, where his colleagues would post them on his Tumblr, *Diario de un preso de conciencia* (diary of a prisoner of conscience).[1] This brought to light Borge's authoritarianism, the dirty dealings of his administration, and the complicity of most of the local press.

As far as Borge was concerned, Pedro had not gotten the message, and continued resistance meant that further action had to be taken against the recalcitrant journalist. The prison rumor mill reported that the inmates "El Picos," "El Payaso," "El Mono," "El Shanghai," "El Coquis," and fifteen others were going to launch an attack from Cellblock 1 to kill Pedro. But Pedro had his own allies on the inside. He'd made friends. "He's a guy who doesn't hurt anyone," said Agustín Chávez, a young immigrant from Honduras, who was in prison for theft. "He helps everyone he can."

Most of Pedro's fellow inmates in Cellblock 2 were there for minor misdemeanors or were innocent victims of an unjust justice system. Among them were a number of fellow Mayans. The justice system was stacked against them. Because Spanish was not necessarily their first language, they might have had a poor grasp of the language and they might not have been provided with trans-lators during their trial. Resolved to protect Pedro, the prisoners of Cellblock 2 positioned themselves in strategic corners near the cellblock's entrance and just outside the reporter's cell, as they urged Pedro to stay strong. Opposed to violence, Pedro had to fig-ure out how to defend himself. He decided to rely on the historic weapon of the press. "I'll use a pencil," he later told me. "I'll make it really sharp and stab anyone who gets in here in the jugular or in the eye."

The courtyard in Cellblock 2 measured around five by twenty meters and was uncovered, except for a set of bars running across it. From the roof, the guards watched the prisoners mobilizing below. Like an audience at the theater before the start of a show, they waited in anticipation. They would not intervene. But if they were eager to see any violence that evening, they would be disap-pointed. The message did get through to Cellblock 1 that "we were ready for them," recalled Chávez, "and to confirm that, the other cellblock sent five people over. When they saw we were going to defend Pedro, they didn't want to come anymore."

Quintana Roo is located on the eastern side of the Yucatan Pen-insula. A state only since 1974, it has seen runaway development and population growth as a result of the huge success of the tour-ist mecca Cancún and other idyllic beaches along the Caribbean coast. It hasn't all been for the good. Take a look beyond the expen-sive hotels and resorts and you will see the steady destruction of the state's delicate natural environment by greedy real estate develop-ers eager to build yet another massive hotel, even as the indigenous Mayan communities are displaced from their ancestral land. This is where Governor Roberto Borge and his unscrupulous politician and entrepreneur cronies established their pirate regime, separating indigenous communities from their land and property with the complicity and assistance of local authorities, who willingly forged signatures and falsified documents. Journalist Lydia Cacho found herself on the receiving end of a number of threats after the website Aristegui Noticias published her investigation on how these land-grabbers would use every possible trick in the book to seize highly valuable land, from buying off judges to forced disappearances and even extrajudicial killing.[2]

This was the region where Pedro grew up, learning to read by studying the labels on the things he saw at the grocery. He was drawn to the camera at an early age after seeing tourists being photographed at the beach. But instead of taking pretty pictures, he felt compelled to take photographs that drew attention to societal injustice—photographs that showed, for example, instances of police corruption. Soon enough, even as he worked selling hot dogs on the street, he started to pass information to reporters. This was during the years when Mario Villanueva was governor, from 1993 to 1999, a time that saw considerable unrest in the area. The Zapatista Army of National Liberation (EZLN), a network formed largely by peoples of Mayan descent, had launched a twelve-day uprising in the state of Chiapas, 600 kilometers away, to improve the miserable conditions created after five centuries of racial domination, first by a White European empire, later by a White-mestizo republic that failed to fulfill its promises. The federal government responded by clamping down on the Zapatistas, which gave Villanueva license to assert his own authority, cracking down on local indigenous leaders in Quintana Roo. Pedro witnessed the governor's abuse of power firsthand and decided to publicly denounce him (since 1999, Villanueva has been in prison for drug trafficking).

Pedro was no stranger to challenging the cozy relationship between the government and the media. He had seen the administration showering journalists with advertising money and various other resources at its disposal in exchange for favorable news coverage. Pedro eventually started a blog that carried his name, in which he started covering local news, and just like Moisés Sánchez, his power lay in finding stories in the local community—which, in Pedro's case, was the historic Mayan community of Carrillo Puerto and its surrounding villages. He would take these stories and help them get picked up by larger media outlets. Otherwise, there was no way the outside world would know what abuses were occurring there. In terms of critical, or even measured, news coverage, the area would have been a black hole.

Carrillo Puerto is a place of great significance to the Mayans. Its original name is Chan Santa Cruz. According to legend, it was here that in 1847 a cross appeared in the trunk of a ceiba tree, which was sacred to the Mayans. From the cross, a voice ordered the people to launch a war of liberation against their white oppressors, the heirs of the Spaniards who had conquered the Yucatán Peninsula in the sixteenth century and had continued to rule over it from the city of Mérida after Mexican independence in 1821.

The Mayans were victorious, which allowed them to found a theocratic state extending from Tulum to Bacalar. They were known as the Cruzoob and were ruled by "singing masters" or "interpreters of the cross," who spoke, it was believed, on behalf of the legendary cross. Carillo Puerto successfully remained independent until its inhabitants were defeated by President Porfirio Díaz's Mexican army in 1901, bringing the racism and brutality the Mayans had rebelled against back to the region.

The revolution that overthrew Díaz's dictatorship never came to the Yucatán peninsula, and the rights assured to most citizens took many decades to reach the Mayans, if they ever did at all. Even now, they have had to endure systemic discrimination, as most indigenous Mexicans do. Pedro gave me an example of how little the authorities cared: in 2014 there had been an epidemic of dengue fever, which barely made the national news. The local government ordered that it remain secret so as not to scare off tourists planning to visit Cancún and the Riviera Maya. This, despite the fact that five thousand people lost their lives to the virus, including Pedro's aunt and cousin. "To them, we're nothing but Indians," he said. "We don't matter." It was business as usual. The rest of the country knows next to nothing about the Mayans of Quintana Roo. So many of them still live in poverty, marginalized by society.

A more recent example was the police repression of indigenous protests in August 2014 over the rising price of water. Like loyal dogs obeying their master's command, most of the state's daily newspapers, such as *Por Esto!*, *Diario Respuesta*, and *Diario de Quintana Roo*, which subsist on funding from the government, avoided crossing the line drawn by the governor's spokesperson and omitted any mention of the protests. But Pedro did cover the protests and posted his reporting online.

The police had attacked unarmed people on August 19 with indiscriminate violence. They had assaulted protestors as well as anyone who just happened to be nearby. "Death to PRI! Death to PRI!" protestors yell in a video uploaded by Pedro. "Long live the peasant struggle! Long live Mayan culture! Death to the bad government!" a group of men shout. "We don't have your jobs, we don't have money!" a woman screams. "Why are you attacking your own people?" shouts another.

Proceso published Pedro's article on the police crackdown. The governor's spokesperson Rangel Rosado fired off a letter accusing him of having provoked a riot with paid protestors. The local press parroted Rosado's accusations, and a judge issued a warrant for Pedro's arrest. He spent five days in hiding but decided to face up to his opponents and hand himself in. "I got angry," he said. "I'm going to fight this."

In a video he uploaded to YouTube on August 24, he directly addressed the governor. "I'm addressing you as my employee because I pay you," Pedro said defiantly to Borge. "I am the people. As my employee you are failing. To save your own dignity you should resign. I challenge you to a debate in the main park. I will wait for you here. I will wait for you here until the north and south poles melt. I hope you come soon. We will have a debate between a citizen employer and the governor employee. Don't be afraid. The Mayans don't eat people. We are peaceful. I invite you."

Pedro had touched on a weak point—Borge's pride. A nephew to Miguel Borge, Quintana Roo's governor from 1987 to 1993, Roberto Borge was born into a wealthy family in the paradise of Cozumel, an island in the Caribbean Sea off the eastern coast of the Yucatán Peninsula. He went to elite Catholic schools, from which he was expelled more than once, before finally attending the leading private university in Mexico, Tecnológico de Monterrey, where he graduated in business administration. Borge attained the governor's office because his predecessor and political godfather, Félix González Canto, thought he was weak and would make for an easily manipulable puppet. He chose Borge as the PRI candidate over Carlos Joaquín, the heir of another influential family. There were many similarities between Borge and Veracruz's Javier Duarte: they both enjoyed privileged education and had the full support of sitting governors. They both rose to power in 2010 and were relatively young to be taking office. Borge was younger: thirty-one to Duarte's thirty-seven. They were the pride of the new PRI, as the party was then marketed. President Peña Nieto was eager to show the international press that the twenty-first-century PRI had broken from its past, free of the stain of its twentieth-century misdeeds. Duarte and Borge were the poster children of this new phase.

Pedro pointed out that, like Duarte, Borge had been subject to bullying throughout his life, his bitterness and insecurity morphing into arrogance, pride, and disdain for those he considered inferior. If Duarte modeled himself after the Spanish dictator Franco, Borge thought of himself as quite a different beast: in January 2016, when a controversy arose with a political rival, he tweeted: "The lion never turns his head when a dog barks." Needless to say, after Pedro issued that challenge to debate him in the park, Borge did not respond. But he would not ignore Pedro for much longer.

If Borge had a sense of humor at all, it was reserved for the people who lived in the major cities. One day in Cancún in May 2012, Norma Madero, director of the weekly magazine *Luces del Siglo*, went to an Oxxo convenience store (one of the few places that sells newspapers and magazines in the state) and noticed that the issue of the magazine on display was not the same as the issue they had printed over the weekend. The cover had been replaced, its headlines rewritten. What had once been a cover story critical of the governor and negative about the state of Quintana showed the governor in a positive light. What's more, this wasn't the only case of swapping out a magazine with a fake issue.

What was done with issues of *Luces del Siglo* may be one day exhibited in a museum of the absurd. Only a few minor changes were made to the covers, mostly limited to the text, but in one instance, the cover had shown a caricature of the governor about to crush his critics with a mallet. The caption had read: "Borge foments terror." This was replaced with: "A strong hand against delinquency," with the word "justice" on the handle of the mallet. In another fake issue, the headline "Borge Ignores Women's Recommendations" was replaced with "Borge Promotes Actions in Favor of Women." The governor clearly needed to convey to the public how close his relationship was to the president, and the covers of magazines were replaced to show images portraying them as allies and friends. One cover featured a photo of Borge and the president laughing together over the tag line "Promises Kept. Quintana Roo Moves Ahead." The changes weren't always restricted to the cover. The headlines and the articles inside the issue were sometimes rewritten to cast the governor in a favorable light. They were always careful to "respect" the reporters who wrote the original article by including their bylines unchanged.

Over four years, forty fake editions of *Luces del Siglo* were printed and distributed in Cancún, as well as thirty more fake digital editions online.

* * *

On August 30, 2014, six days after Pedro uploaded his video challenging the governor to a debate, he was arrested and charged with committing unspecified acts of sabotage against the water system. He was admitted into the city jail in Carrillo Puerto, where "they welcomed me with a beating, the usual." But later that night, some other prisoners carried out what he believes were the orders of Borge and his director of public security, Gerardo Espinoza: "On the rooftop of Cellblock 1 the guards were standing watching, like it was a boxing match, or a play." He was savagely beaten by the prisoners. "They damaged my spine, my rotator cuff, and shoulder blades. They knocked me unconscious." They left him lying on the ground.

The accusation of sabotage leveled against Pedro cannot be substantiated. The only evidence was a photo of the reporter recording police repression at the protest: "My crime was the crime of informing the public," Pedro said. His lawyer, Araceli Andrade, and Article 19 took up his defense. In spite of the case's weakness, six months passed before the defense finally managed to have a judge allow a writ of *amparo*, a legal measure intended to protect citizens from unlawful arrest and human rights violations. This seemed to be a promising development, but then the very same judge suddenly demurred with no explanation. When Pedro asked him why, the judge told him, "This is political. There's an order to lock you up for twenty years. Why don't you find yourself a good negotiator? Why don't you find someone to go talk to the governor and accept his terms? The case will be thrown out and you can get out."

Borge was angry because the outcry over Pedro's case reached national media outlets. At least that is why Pedro thinks Borge ordered the removal of his pencils and pens, with which he wrote the reports that would be posted on his blog. And that's why he laid the groundwork for the attack by the inmates of Cellblock 1. "He ordered my assassination," Pedro said. "They had been planning the attempt. There were rumors they would hang me from the bars so it would look like a suicide. There were a lot of rumors. Your life is at risk just from the adrenaline. It goes up, and up, and it keeps rising. It's still very high to this day, and that leads to anxiety and to depression when the adrenaline drops."

Pedro continued to be a public relations menace for the governor far beyond the confines of his state. Article 19, Reporters Without Borders, and other groups presented the case in international forums. Pedro told me, "A journalist who's killed can't talk, can't defend himself, can't give any clues. The only thing left is pain, and that too is forgotten. It's easier to forget a dead man than forget someone who's alive and suffering."

The governor suffered another blow to his public image when a hacker took control of the Twitter, Facebook, and Hotmail accounts of his spokesperson, Rangel Rosado. The hacker obtained and posted photos and documents showing the fake issues of *Luces del Siglo*. Rosado had used his office to create false information about his political rivals and had these lies published in newspapers favored by government advertising, and the documents revealed that reporters were offered and accepted bribes, and that Borge himself had authorized the operation against Pedro.

Keeping the troublesome Mayan journalist in jail became untenable. In the end, in a sign that the government had, for the time being, failed in its attempt to silence Pedro, he was released.

"I offer up my liberty," he later said, "to all the journalists who were killed for doing independent journalism, to those who did not have the privilege of having a lawyer and an organization supporting them, those who had no way to defend themselves." Even after his release, the threat that Borge could get even in some other way persisted. When Pedro walked out of that prison at midnight on May 28, 2015, two lawyers from Article 19 and the activist group Equipo Indignación escorted him out of the state to the neighboring state of Yucatán, where he boarded a flight to Mexico City. Shortly thereafter he would meet Rubén, Jorge, and Nadia in that restaurant in Roma.

Pedro lamented that over the course of the nine months he had spent in prison he had aged ten years. By outward appearances he had not changed much. He is still strongly built, and the hurt he suffered was not immediately visible. But because of the injuries he sustained while in prison, he will no longer be able to swim down deep in water, as he had always loved to do. When I met him last, Pedro was preparing for surgery, in which metal rods would be implanted in his body. The scars were not only physical, but psychological. They will stay with him for the rest of his life.

A few months after his release, he returned to Carrillo Puerto, even though Borge was still in power. The threats, the harassment, the smear campaigns had all continued against him. But Pedro would not accept defeat. "We can't live in fear. I have to live my life and learn to live with these dangerous circumstances. If they kill me, they kill me, but I won't be their prisoner in my own home, in my own mind."

He told me this while leaning against the bars of his old cell in the prison where he had nearly been killed. The guards had let us in. Although a year had passed, the inmates had not altered the words that Pedro had written on the cell wall. For example, "Jail, a ship that breaks through the waves of time in search of freedom." Although there was only room for four to sleep in the cell, Pedro recalled, "There were six or eight people in here. This is where we washed. This is the bathroom. Here are the brooms. There's my broom. My kitchen utensils are still here. They locked me up physically. They put my body in here. But my thoughts were free."

He had made the decision not to give in. To have faith. Pedro believed he would succeed in getting the judges to call the governor to account: "Justice is coming for Roberto Borge. He will be in a cell just like this one. Revenge is sweet, forgiveness comes in a thousand flavors, all of them delicious, but I would rather have justice."

He held the bars of the cell and looked me in the eye. He seemed to assess the quality of the metal with his hands, gauging their diameter, the solidity with which they hemmed him in. He caressed them lightly, as if a trace of warmth might arise from the smooth, cold metal. Then he let his dark brown arms drift through the bars, almost touching me. He was forty-six, of average height, and a little overweight, with powerful hands and pronounced Mayan features. He said, "It was horrible being here, in this prison, locked up for a lie. It's very complicated. We hope that soon there will be no more impunity in this country, no more locking up innocent people, no more politicians using their power to make up charges and imprison us for the freedom of expression, for thinking. How is it that we are locking people up just for thinking in the twenty-first century, in Mexico?"

We had managed to bring a cell phone into the prison with

Pedro's help and a little bit of luck, hoping that the guards would not make us go through a metal detector. They didn't and we recorded Pedro on video as he told us his story and spent some time in Cellblock 2. The inmates talked and joked around him as they worked on their hammocks. I bought one—it was very well made—for eight hundred pesos.

In the years following Pedro's release, Borge went from being the poster boy for the new PRI to its scapegoat. Journalists had discovered his fraudulent dealings. Mariel Ibarra, of the magazine *Expansión*, and Silber Meza, of Mexicans Against Corruption and Impunity (MCCI), revealed how Borge and his staff had carried out a massive appropriation of real estate and shares of common land owned by businesses and privately, including beautiful beachfront properties on the Caribbean coast and in areas under environmental protection. Eventually, he was indicted for illicit enrichment and money laundering, among other charges.

Like Duarte, Borge fled the country, only to be cornered later. He had been in hiding since November 2016, making his way through eleven countries, including the United States, Cuba, and the Bahamas. His final hideout was a $1,500-a-night room at the Trump Ocean Club International in Panama City before he was captured at nearby Tocumen International Airport, on June 4, 2017, on his way to Paris.

Although the new Quintana Roo government offered a public apology to Pedro in April 2017, Pedro's greatest satisfaction would come later. He was back in his town of Carrillo Puerto, reporting on corruption within the local authorities on his news website, Pedro Canché Noticias, while trying to get his carpentry shop back up and running. He found out Borge had been jailed in Panama's El Renacer Prison, and he flew to Panama and requested an interview through his lawyer. Confusing him with someone else, the lawyer instructed him to buy food, a sweater, and a pair of jeans for the prisoner and bring them the next day. Pedro went along with it.

On June 10, Borge entered the visitor area, expecting to meet his private secretary, Fabián Vallado. Instead he found Pedro.

Pedro remembered the visit vividly.

"Hello, Roberto Borge," Pedro had said, "I've come to visit you.'"

Borge turned pale. He stammered. His jaws were clenched. His face turned red. "He did not expect to see me there," Pedro said. "The governor who had put me in jail at his dictatorial whim was now there . . . defeated. I had never seen him in person, not before or after the time I spent in jail during his administration. I had never seen his face in person. It reminded me of Buzz Lightyear, 'Infinity and beyond,' the character from *Toy Story*."

"Let's talk," Pedro had said to Borge. "This is nothing personal. It's a work of journalism. Tell me how you are."

"I was expecting Fabián. I don't want to talk to anybody. Not to you. What are you doing here?"

Two guards were monitoring the interactions between the visitors and prisoners. Once he had recovered his composure, Borge turned to them. It looked as if he thought he was still in charge. "The arrogance was stunning," Pedro recalled.

"Guard! Get the reporter out of here, please," Borge said. "Have this person removed."

The guard he addressed, a Panamanian soldier, replied, "If you order to have your visitors removed, we won't allow you to have any visitors at all. How will we know which visitors you want, and which visitors you don't? And you know, sir, visitors are respected here. You are within your rights not to accept them. But we do not remove anyone."

El Renacer is a country club prison, holding only those who have paid for the privilege to stay there. According to Pedro, Borge had "a comfortable bed and a plasma-screen TV" in his cell. It was the same prison where General Manuel Antonio Noriega had spent ten years of his life until his death in May 2017, one month earlier. "It's more like a retirement home," said Pedro. Still, Borge had some responsibilities, fellow inmate El Ciervo, serving a sentence for murder, explained to Pedro: "He's responsible for sweeping and cleaning the bathrooms and infirmary. He's already made friends there and asked them to take care of him."

"Is Roberto good with a broom?"

"Yes. Cleaning the bathrooms is harder for him, but he's learning."[3]

5

Proceso

In 2016, *Proceso* celebrated its fortieth birthday. The magazine had been founded in July 1976 as a response to a presidential act of aggression. Then president Luis Echeverría had been traveling the globe in an attempt to position himself as one of the leading heads of state in the Nonaligned Movement, a group of seventy-seven countries refusing to take sides in the Cold War; ultimately he had ambitions to run for secretary general of the United Nations. Still, despite what he said in public, he did not believe in extending the right to freedom of speech to all—especially not to his critics— and he was especially sensitive to any kind of negative coverage at the time, but the daily *Excélsior*, one of the most popular newspapers in Mexico, wasn't towing the line, and its criticism of the president incurred the president's wrath.

Under the PRI, the president had no right to reelection but every right to appoint a successor, and in most cases, he would use this right to play one aspiring candidate against another to test their loyalty and also to stop them from acquiring too much power. The aim was to hold on to power even after stepping down from office. Echeverría thought that his treasury secretary José López Portillo—also his cousin—would be an easily manipulated successor (he was soon proved wrong), but when *Excélsior* published his office's new tax reform proposal ahead of time, it caused serious concern among business leaders, forcing López Portillo to back down. He claimed *Proceso* had taken it from his trash, but the damage had been done. Echeverría's successor was in trouble and the president wouldn't forgive *Proceso*.

Echeverría waited until immediately after the 1976 presidential election and had *Proceso*'s editorial director Julio Scherer dismissed. In a milestone in the history of journalism in Mexico, over two hundred writers working for the newspaper resigned with him in protest. Just four months later, Scherer and his fellow *Excélsior* journalists, including Vicente Leñero, Enrique Maza, and Miguel Ángel Granados Chapa, launched *Proceso* ("process" in English), the left-wing weekly that would come to exemplify investigative journalism and a critical stance toward the ruling party. And it wasn't the only independent magazine to be formed as a result of Scherer's dismissal. The monthly *Vuelta*, which was created by Octavio Paz, and the daily *unomásuno*, founded by Manuel Becerra Acosta, followed *Proceso*.

From the outset, as outlined in the editorial of its inaugural issue, the new magazine's mission was clear: "Founded on facts, processing real events and their protagonists." The editorial read:

> Battered by the political animosities that have stunned Mexico and beyond because of the audacity of the aggression and the high standing of those who have wielded it, we will not make *Proceso* a weekly full of spite and resentment. First, because we understand the political nature of the situation we are in; and second,

most importantly, because of the support and generosity of the vast number of Mexicans who are determined that the nation cannot be completely silenced.

The journalists working for *Proceso* planned to report on politics, business, social issues, and crime, fully cognizant that they ran the risk of retaliation. Many of its scoops are now legendary, and they are a perennial thorn in the side of authorities. As a result, authorities have deliberately withheld information from reporters from the magazine. Reporters have had to endure harassment, persecution, and death threats—some have had to move to a different city or flee the country, some have been abducted, and some, such as Regina Martínez and Rubén Espinosa, have been murdered. The magazine has had its offices ransacked and has been the subject of intensive smear campaigns. In some states, entire press runs have been confiscated and copies burned. *Proceso* is "an anomaly," said respected historian Lorenzo Meyer. "A magazine like *Proceso* shouldn't exist because it was born in the midst of an authoritarian regime, and authoritarian regimes can't allow the existence of independent mass media."

"José López Portillo showed us the path to independence," *Proceso*'s current director Rafael Rodríguez Castañeda told me, with irony. It seemed hard to believe that López Portillo, who was president from 1976 to 1982 and shared his predecessor Luis Echeverría's vastly inflated ego, would have shown the way to a media outlet founded as an act of journalistic rebellion against another president—against all the presidents, in fact. *Proceso* had, after all, throughout his term exposed the many major cases of corruption in his administration, in particular its ties with Jorge Díaz Serrano, director of Petróleos Mexicanos (Pemex).

López Portillo was determined to financially ruin the magazine, and he thought he had the tools necessary to destroy it: since the nineteenth century, the Mexican media industry has grown by living off the government's advertising budgets at the federal, state, and local levels. This has provided news companies their main and sometimes sole source of financial revenue, which in turn guarantees an outsized degree of influence to those who decide who receives the money. Those who align themselves to the official line are rewarded with advertising money, while those who rebel are punished and left to starve. In Mexico, very few media outlets survive off their readerships alone.

Proceso was the first.

At thirty-two, Rodríguez Castañeda had been one of the youngest journalists to leave *Excélsior* along with Scherer and his colleagues, and helped coordinate the founding of the magazine. He recalls how critical a role the public played at the new weekly from day one. For instance, an event for potential investors in the new company was attended by over two thousand people, and the art critic Raquel Tibol persuaded prominent artists to donate works for an auction fundraiser. "*Proceso* bet on becoming a natural, permanent, and fundamental communicator of our editorial line to the readers," said Rodríguez. *Proceso* readers were, and still are, demanding. The same goes for the editors themselves, who still hold themselves to the high standards set by the Scherer generation. "This is in contrast to most media, where the communicator is power."

Public support was vital, because in April 1982 the López

Portillo administration ordered all federal departments, all state governments, and the entire PRI party to cancel their advertising contracts with *Proceso*. Business interests followed suit, with their own boycott in June. The Confederation of National Chambers of Commerce (CONCANACO) told their affiliates and private businesses that "it would be absurd for private companies to give advertising money to publications that want to put an end to the free market." López Portillo himself explained his reasoning at his annual meeting with media executives on June 7, Press Freedom Day: "A commercial company set up as a professional business has the right for the State to give it advertising only to systematically oppose it? This, gentlemen, is a perverse relationship, a gruesome relationship, a sadomasochistic relationship that approaches many perversions that I am not going to mention here out of respect for the audience. 'I pay for you to hit me'? Well, no, gentlemen!"

The notion that the public budget belongs to the president or the officials who administer it lies at the root of corruption in Mexico. Historically, it has been used as a tool to control information. The slogan "*¡prensa vendida!*" (press for sale!), popular at least since the student movement of 1968, has been hurled at corrupt reporters, but also at the most honest ones, in spite of their efforts to rise above the complicity between the largest media outlets and power.

The López Portillo boycott, with support from business interests, "shook the company's finances," Rodríguez Castañeda said, forcing him to close his news agency and lay off workers. "There had been greater revenue from advertising than newsstand sales and subscriptions," he admitted. But a short time later, in one of *Proceso*'s most memorable scoops, the president, who had vowed to "defend the peso like a dog" and then saw it lose almost all of its value, was discovered to have purchased a large hilltop property where he was building four mansions and an ostentatious library. It came to be known as "*la colina del perro*" (the hill of the dog). Because of the story, the magazine increased its print run from thirty thousand to one hundred thousand copies, and with that, the director explained, "*Proceso* learned how to be financially independent through its readers."

The boycott continued, but the magazine managed to build readership through its investigative reporting and by providing alternative perspectives on major events, such as the 1985 earthquake or the political infighting and high-profile assassinations of the early 1990s. Scoop followed scoop, which left the government shaken. Their reporters revealed the existence of the White Brigade, a 240-strong paramilitary group consisting of army and police personnel that used illegal tactics in the 1970s to destroy guerrilla movements. They investigated the luxurious mansions of Arturo Durazo, who terrorized citizens during his tenure as Mexico City police chief from 1976 to 1982, and of Carlos Hank González, the patriarch of the Grupo Atlacomulco, an informal political network of powerful PRI figures who have been very influential in the politics of Mexico State and the federal government. In the mid-1990s, the indigenous Zapatista uprising in the southeastern state of Chiapas was portrayed as senseless banditry by most other media, but *Proceso*'s coverage was in-depth, allowing readers to understand what the rebels wanted to achieve and the poetic mystique behind their demands. Meanwhile, public intellectuals like Fernando del Paso, Francisco Toledo, Marta Lamas, José Emilio Pacheco, Olga Pellicer, and Carlos Montemayor have regularly contributed to its pages, as have some of the best cartoonists, including the late Rogelio Naranjo and Roberto Fontanarrosa. Over the decades, *Proceso* struggled against the system that aligned media with power and was rewarded by their followers.

When Vicente Fox was elected president in 2000, bringing an end to seventy-one years of PRI rule, the boycott remained in place (it would only be lifted in 2019, under López Obrador). The magazine survives off its readership and in close relationship with its readership, and not from official or private advertising. This is what *Proceso* called "forty years of freedom" on its anniversary issue cover, which featured a Gonzalo Rocha cartoon depicting the sour-faced caricatures of eight presidents, from Echeverría to Peña Nieto.

Many of the best-known journalists in the country have been on staff or have collaborated with *Proceso*—most of the journalists profiled in this book can be linked to the magazine—and many *Proceso* journalists went on to found or direct other media outlets. It has been also been a source of inspiration to many other publications. As a result of the watershed in 1976, independent journalism has spawned numerous outlets, from *Vuelta* and *unomásuno* to today's Sin Embargo and Aristegui Noticias. In 1993, the owners of the northern city of Monterrey's daily *El Norte* founded *Reforma* in Mexico City, both with as strong a record for scoops as *Proceso*. Because of *Proceso*, other traditional media, like *El Universal* (where I started doing investigative journalism in 1997) cautiously explored that field. Nonetheless, all of them combined only reach a relatively small portion of the population, who still mainly get their news from the commercial TV networks Televisa and Televisión Azteca, where coverage deviating from the official line is rare. In addition, they have to grapple with the challenge of survival in an environment of prolonged crisis in the industry.

Some journalists who worked for the magazine have also since swapped sides, working for media that are aligned with the ruling party—for instance, Carlos Marín, widely considered one of the great reporters of the early years of *Proceso*. Born in 1947, he had started working as a journalist in 1969 at *El Día* newspaper, which at the time was considered a mouthpiece for the left wing in the PRI. He joined *Excélsior* in 1973 only to leave it three years later with Scherer.

During the 1990s, *Proceso* was seeing its share of internal strife; it was the end of an era. The magazine turned twenty in 1996, and its founders Scherer, Leñero, and Maza announced their decision to retire. A number of candidates vied to take the helm of the magazine, and in the end, it was decided to form a board of directors with six members from the contingent who had followed Scherer from *Excélsior*, including Rafael Rodríguez Castañeda and Carlos Marín. Ongoing professional and personal conflicts, however, led in 1999 to the board asking reporters to elect one editorial director, either Rodríguez Castañeda or Marín. Marín would have none of this. He presented his resignation and went to work for the magazine *Milenio Semanal*.

Milenio Semanal was owned by the powerful Grupo Multimedios, which hailed from Monterrey and owned a newspaper and radio and television stations in that city, where they were direct competition to the daily *El Norte*, owned by Grupo Reforma. The former was close to PRI and the latter to PAN, and both media groups' strategy was to expand into Mexico City to reach a national audience. Multimedios's owners, the González family, had the financial resources to do so. In 2000, they launched *Milenio Diario*, a daily that quickly set up local editions in other states. This was followed in 2008 by Milenio Televisión. All of these came under the general editorial command of Marín. In the beginning, he had had to share a leadership role with journalists Raymundo Riva Palacio and Ciro Gómez Leyva, but that didn't last. He quickly managed to force out the former and subordinate the latter.

Marín had no intention of taking *Milenio* down the same independent path as *Proceso*. On the contrary, he managed to secure its financial stability through a close alignment with the ruling party, whether PRI or PAN. Ethics played no role. A good example of this took place on March 7, 2016, when *Milenio*'s new data journalism unit, led by Karen Cota, performed a statistical analysis of the Peña Nieto administration's most important public assistance program, the National Crusade Against Hunger. She discovered the agency in charge, the Secretariat of Social Development (SEDESOL), had not been doing its job and was reporting false figures. SEDESOL claimed their program benefited 4.17 million people, but according to their own register the actual number was less than a third of that: 1.15 million. Moreover, in the poorest states, the program's coverage of the population living in extreme poverty was very low; in the least poor states, the program's coverage was strangely larger than the vulnerable population itself.

The day after the story ran, Rosario Robles, secretary of agrarian, land, and urban development and formerly of SEDESOL, showed up at *Milenio*'s offices and, pounding on the table, demanded the paper retract the numbers they had published. Marín assigned a reporter to write the document that they attributed to SEDESOL, which provided more favorable figures from a poll by the National Institute of Statistics and Geography (INEGI). The headline was "Crusade Against Hunger did reduce need: INEGI." Robles also ordered the paper to change the headline of the original article from "The (false) success of the National Crusade Against Hunger" to "The success of the National Crusade Against Hunger." Karen Cota resigned from *Milenio* in protest.

Two years later, the Federal Superior Auditors concluded the initiative only assisted 8,696 people, just 0.1 percent of the 7.5 million considered living in extreme food poverty.

During the 2012 presidential election, Enrique Peña Nieto's meticulously planned campaign was imperiled by the youth movement #YoSoy132 (#IAm132), which united students from public and private universities across the country to demand democratic transparency, including in government advertising. As a damage control measure, Peña Nieto announced various compromises, including proposing legal changes so that his administration's media budgets would not be distributed at the discretion of elected office holders, but using clear criteria that prioritized institutional objectives and not individual or party goals.

It did not take long for him to renege on that promise. According to the research center Fundar, the Peña Nieto administration spent almost $2 billion on advertising between 2013 and 2016, in contracts that were awarded to media outlets at the whim of officials. What's more, state and municipal administrations as well as political parties (for which 90 percent of contributions should, by law, come from government budgets) have invested hundreds of millions of dollars to reward loyal media outlets.

Proceso continued its work under the Peña Nieto administration, providing in-depth coverage of events such as the Ayotzinapa movement and other recent social protests, as well as corruption, including that involving the state-owned oil company Pemex, the administration's deals with foreign companies (like Spain's OHL and Brazil's Odebrecht) that bribed their way into construction contracts, the diversion of funds from social programs to political campaigns, the systemic waiving of taxes for large corporations and billionaire businessmen, and the frequent opening of incomplete hospitals and roads. *Proceso* also reported on Peña Nieto's declared pride for "new PRI" poster boys such as governors Javier Duarte and Roberto Borge, and his extraordinary error in judgment when he invited then presidential candidate Donald Trump to a state visit in Mexico.

When Peña Nieto was about to take office, the head of his transition team, Aurelio Nuño, had a coffee with Rodríguez Castañeda at a restaurant in the upscale Polanco neighborhood of the capital. "There's no problem for us," Nuño began. "We simply accept *Proceso* as an enemy."

"I reject that word," the journalist replied. "You can say we're hypercritical, that we don't see anything new in politicians' conduct, but you can't categorize me as an enemy as if we were political rivals, or as if we wanted the public to rise up in arms to topple the government."

Nuño replied: "It's plain and simple. We know you. That's how we'll interact with you. Even enemies can understand each other."

It was clear to Rodríguez Castañeda what was in store for *Proceso* with that administration, "and that's how it's been, but not just with *Proceso*, that's how the government has treated any critical press," he told me back then. "Just look at Carmen Aristegui," referring to the nationally renowned, highly popular journalist and radio host.

The history of *Proceso*, its director continued, "will be the history of the presidential term, its relationship with each one of the presidents, its confrontation with power, revealing what each administration wants to hide, the eternal history of journalism exercised with integrity, with its most essential elements. When *Proceso*'s story is told, nobody could say we have broken our promise, with our founders or with ourselves."[1]

6

Along the Border

In downtown Ciudad Juárez, there is a square called Plaza del Periodista (journalism square), where the devastation caused by gang warfare is readily apparent. No one had cleaned up the walls of a children's party center painted with a scene of Snow White dancing with the Seven Dwarves, and strafed by gunfire and set ablaze some years before. Making any sort of proprietary gesture in a place like this could incite the wrath of someone dangerous. In one corner of the square, there is a small statue dubbed "El Papelerito" (the newsboy). It represents all the boys and young men who sell newspapers in the streets. It was erected as a symbol of freedom of expression, but no sooner had it been unveiled on November 6, 2008, then someone immediately placed a bag at the foot of the statue. It contained a human head. The body was far away, hanging from a highway overpass. The victim was later identified as twenty-three-year-old Sergio Arturo Rentería Robles. Why he was the victim of this crime remains unclear.

El Diario de Juárez journalist Rocío Gallegos remembered that local journalists at the time thought, "They are trying to tell us to shut up, that we are in danger or that someone could get killed. But we didn't get it. There was a little bit of resignation among us, inertia, it was complicated. You don't see the warning signs because you get carried away by this dynamic, this cycle of information and violence."

In 2008, at the beginning of what President Calderón called "the war on drugs," if you wanted to see the direction the country was going in you just had to go to the states along the border of the United States and Mexico—and in particular Juárez, a city in the state of Chihuahua on the border with Texas. Juárez lies more or less at the halfway point along the two-thousand-mile border between Mexico and the United States. The city was the site of a feud between the so-called Cártel de Juárez and the Sinaloa Federation (from which the Juárez Cartel had broken away), and as a result, it was also the site of the first "joint operation" of the army and federal police to oust organized crime and take control of security. President Felipe Calderón was eager to make Juárez a showcase for his new strategy on tackling organized crime. Far from improving the situation, it only grew worse. Violence tore the state apart. There were 15.3 homicides per hundred thousand Chihuahua inhabitants in 2007. By 2011, it had jumped eightfold to 126.1. When I was there working on a story, I spoke with Sergio Belmonte, who was the spokesperson for the city. It was August 2008, which he described as "the worst month in the worst year in the history of Juárez" because of the already unprecedented levels of violence. "This is not normal. You should come back once things are better." But it wasn't going to get better. The chaos had only just begun. And it was clear that he was already afraid. When we parted, I remember he took my hand and said, "I hope you are very careful with my words so it doesn't seem like I said anything compromising, even if I did." There were tears in his eyes. "For my family. You'll see, we'll still be here and they could kill us all."

Belmonte would be arrested two years later, charged with stealing 80 million pesos ($600,000) from the city budget. He was right about the fact that just living in Juárez was extremely dangerous, especially for journalists who did not follow the party line—a line he was in charge of imposing with threats or worse for the administration of PRI mayor José Reyes Ferriz. The danger was greatest for those reporting on criminal activity not only by the gangs but by the police and military.

On November 13, 2008, three months after my visit and just a week after the head was found in Plaza del Periodista, reporter Armando "El Choco" Rodríguez was murdered. They killed him in the morning, in his driveway, while he and his eight-year-old daughter were in the car about to go to school. A gunman approached the driver's window and fired ten shots with a 9-millimeter pistol. Armando was forty years old. The crime left every journalist in the region profoundly shaken.

Assigned in 2007 to the police beat at *El Diario de Juárez*, the leading newspaper in town, Armando, whose nickname "El Choco" came from his brown skin, started by covering one or two stories a day. Rocío Gallegos was the head of reporters in 2008. At the time, she remembers, there were in some weeks "up to twenty homicides a day. It was really alarming, especially because it was not a recognized war zone. In a situation like that, you know who is fighting and what they are fighting over. We knew they were fighting over drug trafficking routes, but we didn't know where, or who." Highly prolific, "El Choco" filed 907 stories in his final eight months on the job, averaging four per day. His death was one of 1,607 homicides in Juárez that year.

Patiently cultivating sources in the police and judiciary, as well as in the criminal organizations, and possessing a fine understanding of who was who and what they did, Armando discovered and documented the infiltration of organized crime into the armed forces. Lucy Sosa, who worked with him, told us how the conflict between the Juárez Cartel and the Sinaloa Federation was replicated in the municipal and state police, who were not only serving these gangs but were often part of them: "The police commanders themselves were leaders," she said. "For example, Sergio Garduño, who's the head of the anti-kidnapping group in the North Zone in Chihuahua and is now a fugitive, he was the leader of Gente Nueva, an armed branch of the Juárez cartel." Armando wrote about shipments of drugs that were confiscated by police and then returned to the traffickers; about military commanders who fabricated cases and manipulated crime scenes to implicate police in rival gangs; and about soldiers who had committed torture.

El Choco's colleagues had to cover their friend's assassination in the paper. Rocío Gallegos remembers "calling the staff together and saying, guys, we have to write the piece, to coordinate coverage. That edition was really hard to do. We gathered together, crying tears of rage, and decided to take a stance as reporters, beyond what the company could say. We decided to tell the community that we were not going to let them stop us, that if they wanted to silence Armando's voice, we were going to amplify it. They had deprived us of our public life, our spaces, but it would be a step backward to let them deprive us of something else, our right to be informed."

While Armando had already been receiving death threats, his colleagues suspected that the motive was related to an article published two weeks before his murder, in which Armando wrote about the nephew of Patricia González, the Chihuahua state attorney general, and his links to organized crime. The investigation shed little light on who had been behind the killing and proved to be fraught for everyone involved. A federal investigator was appointed to Armando's case, but he was killed in July 2009. His successor was also killed, shortly thereafter. As Lucy Sosa later recalled, "Most of the people who participated in the investigation are dead. They were killed, one by one, from the experts and agents from the state public ministry, to the federal public ministry agents who arrived at the crime scene."

In September 2010, President Calderón told a visiting delegation from the Committee to Protect Journalists that the death of Armando had been solved. Two suspects had been apprehended—both of them hitmen for La Línea, squad of police and ex-police working for the Juárez Cartel—and they had both confessed. The attorney general's office followed up by issuing a press release on September 23 with the same information. An hour later, it had been replaced. Some of the information had been removed: the reference to La Línea and the two suspects had changed to only one suspect. Luckily, Gallegos had a copy of the original press release, and she and her colleague went in search of the two men. They discovered that that the one suspect had been found hanged to death in jail three months earlier. The other, Juan Alfredo "El Arnold" Soto, had filed a complaint with the National Human Rights Commission on the day after his confession, saying he had been tortured.

Meanwhile, that same month, gunmen had killed a *Diario de Juárez* intern, photographer Luis Carlos Santiago, who was just twenty-one years old. He had been in his car, with his colleague Carlos Sánchez Colunga, in a shopping mall parking lot where a man had just been murdered. They were both shot from a moving car. The motive was in all probability to deter journalists from covering the crime any further. The following Sunday, the paper published an editorial that addressed the criminal groups directly: "We would like to inform you that we are communicators, not fortune tellers. Therefore, as information professionals we would like you to explain what you want from us, what would you like us to publish or not publish, so we know what to work on. At the moment, you are the de facto authorities of this city, because the legally mandated institutions have not been able to do anything to keep our colleagues from falling, even though we have repeatedly demanded that they do so." Politicians and officials accused the owners of the paper of surrendering to narco-traffickers. Gallegos, who was not involved in conversations that led to the editorial, later explained that it was about "sounding an alarm, to make people look around and see not only the condition journalism was in in Juárez, but the overall condition of Juárez. *Diario* journalists never surrendered and we are still here."

The following month, October 2010, state attorney general Patricia González's brother, Mario González, was abducted. He appeared in a video, handcuffed, with a hood over his head, and held by five men pointing AK-47 and AR-15 rifles at him. Mario says in the video that Patricia was working for La Línea and that she had ordered the reporter's killing. Clearly, his statement was obtained by force and so lacks credibility, but that line of investigation was simply dropped.

In the meantime, journalists were trying to take their security into their own hands. Gallegos, Sosa, and other women journalists like Gabriela Minjares and Araly Castañón were among those who founded the Red de Periodistas de Juárez (Juárez journalists network) in April 2011, following a national trend of creating journalist collectives which surged over the last fifteen years to confront violence, a precarious job market, a lack of training, and corruption in the media. Gallegos says, "we understood that we have to come together, to rise above competition between media companies, to do our job in a more secure way." They offer alternatives to the the Asociación de Periodistas de Ciudad Juárez (Juárez association of journalists) or the Club de Periodistas de México (Mexican press club), which, like so many others, have functioned for decades as public relations support for PRI or PAN politicians, exchanging favors for favorable coverage.

"Who was going to look out for us?" Gallegos asked. "Journalists used to normal circumstances suddenly find ourselves in extreme circumstances. Without realizing it, never having been warned, we were mired in a warlike situation. The city was focused on taking care of itself. We had to protect ourselves." At the same time, they had to continue doing what they do. "If the people keep going, if the people get up to go to work, we journalists cannot stop doing our work. The people of Juárez are not telling us what we have to do. They go out, scared, with caution, but they do go out and go on with their lives." As journalists, they had to stop history from repeating. Sosa, who had to edit the articles on the murders of El Choco and Luis Carlos Santiago, said, "No journalist likes to write about a colleague's murder. It's incredibly painful. It's something you never want to have to do."

In October 2016, El Choco's alleged killer, Juan Alfredo Soto, was sentenced to thirty years in prison. Previously, he had been found guilty of murder in a massacre of sixteen teenagers in the Juárez neighborhood of Villas de Salvárcar, mostly on the basis of confessions he claimed he made under torture. At least three accomplices in El Choco's death have gone uncharged, and as is the norm in Mexico, the authorities declared that justice had been served and refused to investigate any further. The intellectual author of the crime is still at large.

Eight years after El Choco's murder, I visited the offices of *El Diario de Juárez*. Armando Rodriguez's desk and his old computer were kept intact on the upper floor. In his cubicle, like an altar gathering dust, there were photos, flowers, and messages for him. Gallegos, for whom he had worked, had been promoted to general director, the first woman in the newspaper's history to hold that position. She showed me around her murdered colleague's workplace. "He is here," she pointed to his picture, "not physically, but in our discussions, our jokes, our demands."

In the state of Tamaulipas, Los Zetas, a group of elite military officers trained by the United States and lured in 2004 to serve the so-called Cártel del Golfo (Gulf Cartel) as its most-feared hit squad, have been at war with their former bosses since they split in 2010. This feud grew increasingly violent after several of their upper ranks died or were extradited to the United States, and the internal succession battles have provoked further divisions and new rivalries. The state earned the nickname "Mataulipas," playing on the word *mata*, meaning "kill."

The epicenter of fear was the municipality of San Fernando, where some of the most horrifying crimes have taken place, including the mass execution of seventy-two Central American migrants in August 2010, and the discovery in April 2011 of forty-seven clandestine graves containing the remains of 193 people, all of them with their skulls smashed with what appear to be hammers. Most of them had been traveling by bus through the area when they were abducted, as journalist Marcela Turati wrote: "San Fernando is the site of a migrant holocaust. And it's not only migrants who have suffered. The people of San Fernando have been targets, too. The reasons are manifold. It could be because someone saw or heard too much. It could also come down to a person's beauty or wealth or their age—young men of a recruitable age are vulnerable. It could be because someone was suspected of being *contrarios*, providing services to the rival Gulf Cartel. It could be because a business owner refused to provide services to soldiers deployed here or because someone has missed the 6 p.m. curfew."[1] Whatever the reason, Los Zetas and the local police who aided them were behind the killings.

People say there are many more bodies still buried, from three to six thousand. The economy has been ravaged by the ongoing instability. Racketeering, extortion, kidnapping, and murder have forced the closure of most businesses. Farmers have abandoned their fields of sorghum, the region's main crop. Many have had to leave the area, and their empty houses can be spotted throughout the region. Those residents who remain have been neutralized by fear. They cannot protest under the threat of death.

Regions along the border abound with stories that journalists can uncover and report only at enormous risk because politicians, police, and business interests, in association with organized crime, always keep them under close watch. In Tamaulipas, the authorities have managed to impose a media blackout. Information about the ongoing violence there never sees the light of day or else it is micromanaged.

Borrowing language from the military, criminal organizations call cities "plazas," and their local commanders are "plaza chiefs." They appoint press handlers, known as *enlaces*, (liasons) to dictate to reporters, editors, and media owners what they should and shouldn't publish. These *enlaces* generate their own content, both articles and photographs, which they send to the press with detailed instructions, such as the page number and position where they should be printed. They also recruit people who are on staff at the newspaper—messengers, reporters, managers, and even security personnel—who keep them informed of everything going on at the paper in exchange for money, or simply under threat of death. Add to this the pressure by the Peña Nieto administration to suppress negative stories. Political columnist Martín Moreno has repeatedly shown how the general director of Grupo Imagen, Ernesto Rivera, prohibited stories about Tamaulipas in the daily *Excélsior*, in spite of the critical situation in the state.[2]

In Reynosa, local television reporter Miguel Turriza told me what it's like to live under constant threat, as we walked along the edge of the Río Bravo. He has had to learn not to broadcast any more information than is prudent, since "they know where we live, they know where our kids go to school, they know where we work. Eight friends or people I knew in the media, especially working on public security, disappeared, they were never seen again. And even after those disappearances, some of us kept on reporting until we realized we couldn't anymore. Before, we would go, 'Hey, something's going on, a shoot-out'; we tried to get close and see what was happening, like we normally would. Not anymore," because "our media offices were bombarded, shot at. Until recently, we couldn't even go out in the street."

Further complicating things, with fighting among rival criminal organizations exacerbated by internal divisions, reporters find themselves caught in the crossfire. Erick Muñiz and Melva Frutos of the Red de Periodistas del Noreste (journalists network of the northeast) explained this in Monterrey. "When just one group is in charge, there's no problem, you listen to them and it's over," said Muñiz, but "the serious situation is when there's two groups. Then one says 'publish this' and the other says 'don't publish that.' One of them is going to be mad at you. And sometimes, there's a third."

If that wasn't enough, the whims of these groups go beyond crime stories and seep into frivolous subjects, Frutos added. They berate you "because you covered that baby's baptism, and not mine, my son; or that quinceañera, but not the one for this capo's daughter. In a children's sports league, you covered the baseball game of the son of that capo, but not my son, on the other team."

Enrique Juárez Torres was no stranger to the risks of being a journalist in the region. For several years, the daily *El Mañana*, which had survived grenade attacks and shootings of its offices, published stories in each of its local editions in Matamoros, Reynosa, and Nuevo Laredo, which border Brownsville, McAllen, and Laredo in Texas respectively, following the orders of the area's dominant criminal leaders.

Juárez was the editor in chief of the Matamoros edition of *El Mañana* when, on November 5, 2010, the Mexican Navy mobilized 180 troops to capture Antonio Cárdenas Guillén, or "Tony Tormenta," the leader of the Gulf Cartel in Matamoros. For eight hours, it was urban warfare. People's homes were used as battlements for snipers. The gunfire was constant. Everything was shut down, including the three international border bridges to Brownsville. Juárez said, "It was like a horror movie." According to official reports, three navy troops, an army soldier, and four gang members were killed, including Tony Tormenta, and the press "link." But information control was so important for the Gulf Cartel, that by nine o'clock that evening they had already named a new "link," who was instructing the media "not to publish the name Tony Tormenta in any Matamoros newspapers." "And no one did," Juárez recalled.

Five years later, the owners of the paper decided it was time to put an end to their submission to the gangs. They saw their chance in early February 2015, after a fierce three-day street battle between two rival factions of the Gulf Cartel erupted in Matamoros and elsewhere in the region. The newspaper owners directed staff to publish a story about the violence in the local edition. Juárez followed the instruction, and when the papers went on sale the next morning, February 4, panic spread among employees—the *enlace*'s informant was especially worried—because they knew the story would bring consequences.

The article was on the front page. The office was flooded with phone calls from unknown numbers. Juárez did not answer any of them. That afternoon, two men burst into the *El Mañana* offices and went up to the second floor in search of Juárez. They grabbed him and dragged him down the stairs and into a van, kicking and shouting at him while driving around the city. "I thought they were going to kill me," Juárez recalled. "I asked them, 'Are you going to kill me?' When they said no, I relaxed," even though he knew he was going to be beaten within an inch of his life. "They asked me why I published that article and if I knew I shouldn't have. They were punching me all over my body. They seemed to want to leave marks on my face, so I was trying to protect my face. 'Don't cover your face!' they yelled." They told him they would kill him if he continued to publish articles on violence in the area, before taking him back to his office.

This was by no means an unusual occurrence. My Ojos de Perro colleague Juan Castro interviewed a journalist in another part of Tamaulipas, who asked to remain anonymous, since he would suffer reprisals if it was discovered that he had talked about this. "I have been attacked by criminal groups twice," he said. "It's an experience you wouldn't wish on anybody, the simple fact that they have you on your knees, with a gun to your head, telling you they're going to blow your fucking brains out. You think of your family, sometimes you wonder if being a reporter was worth it, you see your life flash in front of you. Then comes the beating, and you kind of think, well, all right, at least they didn't kill me."

This resignation to physical punishment has almost become a job requirement. Sooner or later, you're going to get "picked up" and reprimanded. On at least one occasion, explained Juan Alberto Cedillo, *Proceso* magazine correspondent for northeastern Mexico, in 2014 a criminal organization named a new *enlace* who, just to make it clear who was in charge, ordered all the crime reporters working in Ciudad Victoria, the capital of Tamaulipas, to be brought to him to give them a "paddling." They were stripped naked, hung up by their hands, and their buttocks beaten with what a witness described as "a big piece of wood, two inches thick, with holes in it, so the air passes through and it makes a stronger impact."

The anonymous journalist, who is from another city, suffered this same "paddling" when they came after him because of "a regular article, innocuous, a commentary, which didn't affect anything. But somebody felt offended, and they knew this gangster, and that was it, all of a sudden, they got me. I was in intense pain, my flesh all cut up, for almost three weeks, my buttocks and part of my legs all bloody." Getting "paddled" is not the only possible punishment. Others include getting the "hands" (slapped around), the "bonfire" (burns on the skin), the "scissors" (cutting off body parts), and the "ground" (killed).

"What they did to me was a warning," Juárez said. "It is a warning to all of us who work there, those who are physically in Matamoros and those who are not in Matamoros." He added, "The Matamoros paper will once again avoid publishing stories that could upset the cartel." The following day, the newspaper carried no mention of Juárez's abduction.

After the men brought Juárez back to the newspaper's office, he went back up to the second floor. "One of my coworkers, one of the many who quit right after that, told me, 'You have to get out of here, Mr. Enrique.' I told her no, they already did what they came here to do, no way they're going to say, 'Oh, shit, we forgot to kill him.' They just came to deliver their message and that was it."

But that same night, Juárez and his family crossed the border into Texas. Luckily for him and his family, they all had visas allowing them to enter the United States immediately. They didn't have to apply for asylum. That is not the case for most journalists who are at risk of being killed. (Of all Mexicans who apply for political asylum, 88 percent are rejected.[3] There is no indication that journalists face better odds.) They didn't have to risk their lives crossing the desert. They didn't have to suffer the fate of reporter Martín Méndez, who had fled Mexico in fear of his life but returned after spending a hundred days in Immigration and Customs Enforcement (ICE) detention centers, "because they have deprived me of my freedom with no reasonable response regarding the denial of my release," he wrote in a letter to the judge in charge of his case. "The mistreatment, abuse and humiliations every day became more intolerable."

Maybe he lacked the perseverance necessary to reach his goal. Maybe he should have waited just a bit longer. Emilio Gutiérrez fled Chihuahua after Lieutenant General Ildefonso Martínez Piedra and General Alfonso García Vega of the Mexican Army threatened to kill him for publishing a series of articles about the military's abuse against civilians. In one 2005 article, he revealed how a group of soldiers in uniform, led by local thug Mabeto Amaya, had broken into the hotel La Estrella in Puerto Palomas, on the New Mexico border, and robbed all the guests. Officers summoned him and demanded he stop reporting on their activities. He filed a complaint at the National Human Rights Commission and wrote a piece headlined "Members of the Military Threaten Reporter's Life." In 2008, soldiers raided his home in the middle of the night, holding him and his fourteen-year-old son down against the ground. They said they were looking for drugs. Again, he filed a complaint and wrote an article. A friend warned Gutiér-rez that the order to assassinate him had already been issued. He and his son decided to cross into Texas and there they began the endless process in which they had to appeal various judicial deci-sions and were detained for six months. His cause won the support of the National Press Club, which awarded him the John Aubu-chon Press Freedom Award. After receiving this honor, he and his son were detained once again in December 2017.

In May 2018, the Knight-Wallace Fellowships for Journalists at the University of Michigan offered a press freedom fellowship to the fifty-five-year-old Gutiérrez, which helped get him and his son released, three months later, and allowed them to travel to Michigan. It seems like a happy ending, but the asylum applica-tion was rejected in March 2019, on the grounds that he didn't prove that his and his son's life were in danger. They have appealed the decision.

Information is a social necessity. The shutting down or censorship of newspapers leaves a vacuum that citizens rush to fill, report-ing on what professional media outlets will not. They denounce the violence and plan events on Facebook, Twitter, and other platforms, but at great personal risk. They form advisory groups to provide information on the troubles they are facing, through websites with names like Courage for Victoria City or Warning Mante City. The best known was Valor por Tamaulipas ("courage for Tamaulipas," known by its acronym in Spanish, VxT), which became a news source for journalists. The gangs decided it needed to be silenced, and in February 2013, they announced a reward of 64,000 pesos that was eventually raised to 3 million pesos to whoever "provides exact information on the owner of the website or their immediate family members, whether they are parents, siblings, children, or a spouse. This is just freedom of expression but in exchange for a nice payment to shut up those big *panochones* [a reporter identified by criminals] like these assholes who think they're heroes." They had no qualms about listing a cell number to contact.

The VxT administrators protected their identities carefully because they knew the threat was all too real. But thirty-nine-year-old journalist María Elizabeth Macías was caught in 2011. She left VxT to write under a pseudonym, "La Nena de Laredo." She was identified by Los Zetas as one of the administrators of the website Nuevo Laredo en Vivo (Nuevo Laredo live). The website denied this, but on September 24, her decapitated body was found next to a computer keyboard, a CD player, several cables, and a note that read:

> OK Nuevo Laredo Live and social media. I am La Nena de Laredo and here I am for my reports and yours . . . for all you who don't want to believe it, this happened to me because of my actions, for trusting the army and the navy . . . Thank you for your attention. Sincerely: "La Nena de Laredo" . . . ZZZZ.

The late Mike O'Connor, then the Committee to Protect Journalists representative for Latin America, wrote: "I believe she did not evaluate the magnitude of her messages. I think she saw it as a personal cause. I believe when she saw what was happening on social media, she committed to reporting in those media. It was a way to be free, to be a journalist in spite of the silence. She must have felt frustrated as a citizen and as a journalist."

The murder of Macías, who was managing editor of the local daily *Primera Hora*, went unmentioned in her own paper.

Tijuana, in Baja California, is located at the end of the US-Mexico border, where it meets the Pacific Ocean. To the north of the city lies San Diego, California, in the United States, separated from Tijuana by a tall, metal fence. This is the site of the busiest land border crossing in the world. On any given day, around seventy thousand people drive north through San Ysidro and around twenty thousand people cross on foot each day, with the same number heading in the opposite direction. It's a major smuggling route: of drugs, people, arms, chemicals, money, metals. It's a city of opportunity and danger.

The weekly newspaper *Zeta* is run out of Tijuana. Its current director is Adela Navarro. Of medium height, with large brown eyes and a measured smile, she can be an intimidating presence. Her reputation certainly precedes her. Born in 1968, she has spent her whole professional life at *Zeta* since joining at the age of twenty-one. Recently, she celebrated her fiftieth birthday as a highly respected journalist, known for her strength, her intelligence, her honesty, and her courage—which some might call rashness. Her bravery in representing the weekly has earned her recognition, such as the International Press Freedom Award, which she received in 2007, four years before Javier Valdez received the same award.

Unsurprisingly perhaps for a news magazine based in one of the most dangerous cities in Mexico, *Zeta* has a blood-soaked past. Navarro took on its directorship from its co-founders, Jesús Blancornelas and Héctor Félix Miranda, or "El Gato" (for "Felix the cat"). Both died in the line of duty.

Blancornelas, who would go on to become one of modern Mexico's most highly respected and admired journalists, was born in the city of San Luis Potosí, in 1936. He had been working in a garage until, at the age of eighteen, he was given the opportunity to cover sports at the newspaper *El Sol de San Luis*. "It was the best beginning you can have in journalism because it wasn't only about providing information, you taught yourself how to comment on and analyze what is happening," he said. He didn't attend journalism school because "journalism schools weren't invented yet," he said. In 1973, then living in Mexicali, Baja California, he covered corruption and the drug trade, which caused him to be dismissed from three different positions before he founded the statewide daily *ABC* in 1976. The federal government was not pleased. They were used to dealing with media magnates who could help deflect criticism. They weren't used to dealing with journalists, and "and our paper was made up of journalists," he said.

"El Gato" started writing for *ABC* shortly after its founding, and he succeeded in angering President José López Portillo with his criticism of his administration. The authorities ordered the troublesome journalist to be fired, but Blancornelas refused. Just two and a half years after *ABC* was launched, a fabricated labor dispute prompted an elite police unit to take possession of the paper's offices. Blancornelas lost the daily, was falsely accused of fraud, and went into exile in San Diego.

From there, Blancornelas and El Gato plotted their next move.

The letter *Z* would later strike terror because of the criminal gang that adopted it, but in 1980, it had no such connotation. It made sense that, since the newspaper that was shut down had taken its name from the beginning of the alphabet, the weekly founded that year would take its name from the end: *zeta*, the name for *Z* in Spanish.

Blancornelas and El Gato were cautious about running the new magazine out of Tijuana. They did not want it to suffer the same fate as *ABC*. Moreover, the state had a monopoly over the production and importing of paper, which it used to control the media. The two journalists therefore decided to keep print operations in San Diego and import *Zeta* into Tijuana, sometimes smuggling issues across the border to avoid reprisals. The magazine quickly became a leader in investigative journalism, digging up dirt on a tightly woven network of politicians, police officers, and crime. It was a journalistic lodestar in a country where the only press that seemed to matter was located in Mexico City. As such, they provoked the ire not only of Jorge Hank Rhon, casino mogul turned politician, but also of the criminal organizations that had set up shop in the westernmost reaches of the border. Initially it was the turf of a branch of the Sinaloa Federation, but that branch broke away and became the so-called Cártel de Tijuana, or Cártel Arellano Félix after its leaders' last name.

Born in 1956, Jorge Hank Rhon was the prodigal son of one of Mexico's most powerful and wealthiest families. His father, Carlos Hank González, was governor of Mexico State from 1969 to 1975, after which he was appointed the regent—effectively the mayor—of the Federal District, which is the heart of Mexico City. He was widely seen as one of the old guard of the PRI and a head of Grupo Atlacomulco, a clan-like faction made up of powerful figures in the party and based in the namesake city in the Mexico State. Jorge's elder brother Carlos, though in business, became involved in politics and was himself part of the PRI aristocracy. Jorge, meanwhile, had developed a reputation as a playboy with a taste for violence and was placed in charge of one of the family's farthest-flung business enterprises, the Agua Caliente racetrack in Tijuana. In Tijuana, he launched Grupo Caliente, a gambling and online betting center, and was also elected mayor of Tijuana and almost made it to the governor's office.

Jorge was initially on good terms with El Gato, but it was perhaps inevitable that their relationship would sour. The reporter, who wrote the satirical column "A Little Something," started to pay attention to the business magnate's excesses, both in public life and private, called him a *pirrurris* (the spoiled son of a wealthy family), and mocked him by exposing his profligate lifestyle of cocaine and women and by predicting that he would run the racetrack into the ground financially. Jorge could not forgive this.

On April 20, 1988, El Gato left his home at nine in the morning, as usual, driving his Crown Victoria. The neighbors had noticed that Victoriano Medina, an employee of Jorge's, had been monitoring the reporter's movements. Medina blocked El Gato's car with his own. Antonio Vera Palestina was in the passenger seat of a truck that drove up behind the Renault, stopped at the driver's window, and shot the reporter in the head with a 12-gauge shotgun.

His readers carried his coffin through the streets of Tijuana and held demonstrations demanding justice. Blancornelas accused Jorge Hank Rohn of orchestrating the killing, but the official investigation came to nothing, halted—some believe—at the behest of Jorge's father. But in 1989, when PRI lost the Baja California elections for the first time in sixty years, the new governor, who belonged to the PAN party, vowed to solve the case. The state prosecutor brought charges against Vera Palestina, Jorge's chief bodyguard, and Victoriano Medina and Emigdio Nevárez, two security guards who worked at the Agua Caliente racetrack. Nevárez, however, was killed in 1992—or as Adela Navarro puts it, "was disposed of." The other two were sent to prison.

There was no official investigation into who could have been behind the crime. Blancornelas couldn't find a lawyer willing to risk his life by taking over the case, and anyhow he was having second thoughts about whether or not he should continue running the paper. It was too dangerous. Francisco Javier Ortiz Franco, an editor at *Zeta* who had legal expertise, convinced him to carry on and volunteered to help him pursue justice for El Gato's murder.

Their days, however, were numbered. On November 27, 1997, Blancornelas was ambushed in his car by a dozen men two blocks away from the *Zeta* offices, on Chula Vista Street. Investigators found eighty shell casings at the scene of the attack. Blancornelas's driver, Luis Valero, who had been fatally injured in the gunfire, managed to put the vehicle in reverse, which saved the journalist's life. Blancornelas was himself shot four times, with one bullet piercing his lung.

Blancornelas was assigned a security detail and was obliged to use an armored car. He longed for the freedom to do his work as a journalist, but he didn't give up: in 1999, he started writing a column that soon was published in thirty-one cities in Mexico. "For five minutes, I didn't die," he told journalist Erick Muñiz. "I have one great advantage, and that is age. Were I younger, I wouldn't have enjoyed or suffered life as I have already." He retired in 2005, afflicted by stomach cancer and the lasting damage from the injury to his lung. Until the end, he never stopped working to consolidate his legacy: "I've worked to make *Zeta* into an institution so that it doesn't end if I'm missing." He died on November 23, 2006, ten days after he turned seventy and four days before the anniversary of the attack.

Meanwhile, Francisco Ortiz's life was also tragically cut short. In June 2004, on leaving a physical therapy clinic with his two children, aged nine and eleven, masked gunmen pulled up next to his car and shot him four times in the head and neck. Jorge Hank Rhon once again fell under suspicion, but nothing happened. No one was charged for the murder.

Blancornelas's attackers were members of San Diego's Logan Heights Gang, which served the Tijuana Cartel's Arellano Félix brothers. A $250,000 contract was placed on his life by Enedina Arellano Félix, the criminal band's boss. Only one of them, Marco Arturo Quiñones, went to jail, but he was eventually acquitted. Another of the attackers, Alfredo Araujo, is also in prison but not for the attack on Blancornelas. He was implicated in the murder of bishop Juan Jesús Posadas and six other people in 1993 in Guadalajara. "Brothers Benjamín, Ramón, and Javier Arellano Félix, the intellectual authors of the crime, weren't even called to account," ran an editorial in *Zeta*.[4]

A full-page photo of El Gato looking straight at the camera has appeared inside the pages of *Zeta* every week without fail since 1988. "Jorge Hank Rhon," reads the accompanying text, as if El Gato were speaking, "Why did your bodyguard, Antonio Vera

Palestina, kill me?" Below that, there is a list of all the governors of the state of Baja California who have done nothing about the case. The text continues: "El Gato asks the current governor [now Jaime Bonilla], 'Can your administration catch the people who ordered my killing?'"

The *Zeta* offices are a few blocks from the Agua Caliente race-track, where Vera Palestina was chief of security. Jorge Hank Rhon organized a big welcome party to greet him at the airport when he was released from prison, having served twenty-seven years for El Gato's murder, and gave him his old job back.

The weekly is a frequent target of harassment, but recently, the journalists at *Zeta* have started to see threats of physical attack. In October 2017, what *Zeta* describes in an article as a "binational intelligence group" set up to persecute organized crime warned the magazine that a Logan Heights Gang member, José Roque, was back in Tijuana. The Sinaloa Federation had, in the mean-time, expelled the Arellano Felix Cartel from Tijuana, and Roque was back to reestablish the group in the city. Among Roque's plans was "to destroy the *Zeta* building with a bomb."[5] A year before, the CJNG was thought to be planning an attack on *Zeta*'s offices after the paper published pictures of the ten most wanted local criminals, eight of them members of the organization. While Arellano Felix was allied to CJNG, in Roque's case, Arellano Félix was working independently.

To protect reporters, articles containing sensitive information are printed under the byline "Zeta Investigations." Navarro says that measure "has worked," although she acknowledges that it has had some negative effects, "because then instead of threatening one person, they threaten three or four, or the editors or co-directors. But now they don't know what's going on, they don't know who is investigating them." Which is to say, if someone is offended by *Zeta* and cannot identify the reporter investigating them, then she is the woman who comes to mind. The directorial chair she sits on now feels too hot, as it was previously occupied by men who suffered assassination attempts. Does she worry?

"I don't think about it," she told me. "I don't want to sound irresponsible either, because I'm not. I am very committed to what I do, very passionate about investigative journalism. But I am thinking about the current issue, and the one after that. I'm thinking about my colleagues, and the work they're doing. The day I start thinking about it, maybe the editorial direction will change, because I could get scared. I try to concentrate on what we're doing."

During the years she has worked there, Navarro's passion for journalism has not abated. "This excites me, having worked with people like Jesús Blancornelas, like Francisco Javier Ortiz Franco, who were my mentors in journalism, who filled us with that hunger for investigative journalism. It's an experience that has really strengthened us. . . . I don't regret a thing. I would do it all again." If she could stand before her twenty-year-old self, just starting on her career at *Zeta*, she would give her a reassuring smile "and tell her to go for it."

She is acutely aware of the toll it has taken. "It has wounded us a great deal. We have been through so much, and it has marked our lives. . . . This weekly has cost lives. It has cost blood. We have had threats, political and fiscal pressure, attacks on morale, everything, in an attempt to get us to stop. It's cost us all of that. But we go ahead, to the next edition, and the next edition, and the next edition. Right now, we're working on the edition that will come out tomorrow, and tomorrow we'll start working on the one for next week. That's our commitment to our readers, to our society, and to journalism. Nothing more."

7

Laura Castellanos

On January 6, 2015, shortly before 8 a.m., nine armed civilians traveling in three pickup trucks ambushed a convoy of twenty federal police vehicles on the streets of the small city of Apatzingán in the western state of Michoacán. It was a poorly planned attack and all of the attackers died in the fray. In fact, the attackers were the only fatalities. Even though they had the advantage of surprise, they succeeded in only wounding two police officers. What's more, only two of the nine were shot by bullets fired by the police. Six others lost their lives in friendly fire. How the ninth man died was unclear.

This was the version of events provided by the federal commissioner for security and integral development of Michoacán, Alfredo Castillo, to the daily *El Universal*, which published it on January 10. It was based on statements from twelve police officers, ballistics analysis, and the autopsies. There was also video from four traffic cameras that recorded what happened, but only brief segments of these were released, showing police assisting the wounded. There were no civilian witnesses, Castillo claimed, because the shootings happened so early in the day, at 7:45 a.m., and there was no one on the Avenida Constitución de 1814, despite the fact that it was one of the city's two most heavily trafficked thoroughfares. No attempt was made to identify the aggressors.

Two days later, Castillo gave a press conference in which he announced that forty-four people had been arrested in relation to the attack—for conspiracy and possession of firearms, including thirteen rifles and grenades. He also elaborated on the official version of events, explaining what had happened to the ninth victim: he had been run over in another incident hours earlier. He confirmed, too, that six had died in friendly fire, and denied reports that there had been other casualties, let alone executions. Charts, videos, and photographs were produced to show the press that the attackers had fired on each other. "Practically all of the people killed could have been fatally shot by members of their own team," he said, "and two people were shot by the federal police as well as by members of their group. Those were fatal wounds so it is impossible to determine which of the bullets caused their deaths. We are not dealing with homicide on the part of the authorities, nor did the police abuse their authority. It was a legitimate form of self-defense."

Castillo angrily dismissed questions from reporters who had later come to the scene. They pointed out that the alleged trajectories of the bullets were highly improbable; that there were, in fact, witnesses; that the nine dead had been killed execution style (the daily *Reforma* reported three unarmed people had been killed; the Associated Press indicated the victims had not fired, they had surrendered and begged for their lives before being gunned down); and that they had seen videos of police altering the crime scene, moving bodies—including those of children—and placing guns near the victims so it looked like they had fired them.[1] There was no way Castillo's account of the attack was accurate—not to mention that he ignored an earlier outbreak of violence that very morning, in which a peaceful protest had been brutally crushed by police, and this earlier incident had been the reason for the gunfight shortly before 8 a.m.

In January 2014, a year earlier, the authority of Michoacán governor Fausto Vallejo's administration was being seriously undermined by the violent crime engulfing the state and accusations that it was linked to Servando Gómez, "La Tuta," the head of the Caballeros Templarios (Knights Templar) gang. As a result, President Enrique Peña Nieto decided to take over public security in Michoacán and named Alfredo Castillo his commissioner, an ad hoc position that quickly came to be dubbed the Viceroyalty. But his appointment brought little stability to the state, and Castillo, who had served as Mexico State's head prosecutor when Peña Nieto was its governor, was soon faced with accusations of authoritarianism, of human rights abuses against the public, and of protecting La Tuta's enemies, CJNG. Irrespective of the truth of these accusations, the influence of the Caballeros Templarios was waning, which benefited the CJNG, allowing it to make its way into Michoacán unopposed.

Castillo's approval ratings plummeted, hitting rock bottom with the shootings in Apatzingán. Calls for Castillo's resignation multiplied. The federal elections were less than five months away; concerned that his presence would have an adverse effect on the elections, the federal government went into damage control, and Secretary of the Interior Miguel Ángel Osorio removed Castillo on January 12.

To the authorities, that should have put an end to the scandal:

they had delivered to the public the head they had demanded. They didn't see any need to do anything more than that. As usual, they thought they could ensure the official story would prevail just by doggedly sticking to it. If facts emerged that contradicted the official account, those would simply cause confusion without any resulting legal or political consequence.

One journalist, unsatisfied with the narrative that had emerged so far, was determined to find out what really happened. Laura Castellanos, a freelancer with an excellent track record and the author of a key book on insurgent organizations, *México Armado: 1943–1981* (armed Mexico: 1943–1981), had spent several years covering violence in Michoacán for *El Universal*, and she was assigned by the paper's editorial director, Francisco Santiago, to travel to Apatzingán to investigate. She and Salvador Frausto, chief of *El Universal*'s investigative journalism unit, discussed a strategy. They knew that several local residents had videoed the events on their cell phones from nearby rooftops. Rumors were going around about the existence of a video that clearly showed what had happened, and that the police, the military, and gang members were looking for it. Frausto and Castellanos decided that she should find it first.

It was a challenging and complex undertaking. Accompanied by videographer Luis Cortés, Castellanos began her investigation, pursuing every lead with extraordinary thoroughness, in Apatzingán and its surroundings, talking to everyone she encountered. She eventually managed to contact some eyewitnesses—the very eyewitnesses who former commissioner Castillo had said did not exist. She also learned about the brutal methods employed by the police and military in their search for the same video material. Families of the casualties were relentlessly harassed, and in one case, state police officers burst in on a private gathering in which relatives were mourning five of the victims, all members of the same Madrigal family. The police took two women and a man into custody, where they were tortured, presented to the press as drug dealers, and imprisoned. A month later, Juan Carlos Rodríguez, "El Oso," who apparently witnessed the massacre, was abducted and killed by unidentified assailants. Such was the fear that many people in the area decided to move to other states to avoid being detained and interrogated.

The video remained elusive. But in their search, they uncovered important information and interviewed key people who helped to reconstruct the events in detail. Frausto remembers Castellanos calling him several times to ask for more time. He was worried, since she was venturing into very dangerous places looking for extremely sensitive material. When she asked to see medical records for the victims of January 6, Dr. Carlos Torres, director of Ramón Ponce hospital, flatly turned her down. "They'll kill me," he warned, "and they'll kill you." She managed to track down one of the most feared organized crime leaders in the region, and one of the most wanted by police: Nicolás Sierra, alias "El Gordo Coruco," a leader of the organized crime syndicate Los Viagras, which had grown in power under Castillo, and organizer of the protest that was crushed by the police in Apatzingán.

Back in Mexico City, Castellanos and Frausto reviewed what they had found, including more video, audio, documents, and, most importantly, thirty-nine statements recorded on audio and video—including one from El Gordo Coruco—that allowed them to put together the puzzle pieces that Alfredo Castillo, the federal police, and the army had wanted to separate.

Their investigative report was ready on February 19, and yet, two months later, *El Universal* still had not published it. Founded in 1916 as a mouthpiece for a liberal faction in the Revolution, *El Universal* remains a leading newspaper, and its website keeps its place as the most visited Mexican website. "The owner is reviewing it," the paper explained to Castellanos and Frausto every time they asked about their story. Having owned *El Universal* since 1969, Juan Francisco Ealy did not micromanage the editorial department, but no major decision was made without his approval, and the case of Castellanos and Frausto's story had serious implications for the federal government's prestige, which had already been shattered by human rights and corruption scandals. Aside from the normal concern the journalists felt about their work receiving the treatment it deserved, they also felt a keen sense of urgency and a rising fear that someone (maybe those most interested in blocking the story's publication) might act against them in an effort to kill the truth. The subjects of an investigative report that paints them in an unflattering light can seek revenge after a story's publication, but it's rare: once a story is out in the open, they would probably rather avoid stirring up more trouble. But if they learn about the story ahead of publication, they will do their utmost to nip it in the bud. For the journalists, the way to neutralize that threat is to publish the story as soon as possible.

But *El Universal* did not seem to be in any rush. As the weeks passed, reporters in the investigative journalism unit—a group in which I was included—and its affiliates felt increasingly uncomfortable over what we viewed as censorship. We suspected that someone at the newspaper had leaked the story to the authorities, which put our colleagues who had worked on it in grave danger. It looked to us like the paper was trying to bury the story. We thought the person behind this was the deputy editorial director, David Aponte, who more than a few of us considered Peña Nieto's man at *El Universal*.

Throughout this process, Castellanos and Frausto found themselves followed. They were being watched, their movements tracked. The surveillance was meant to scare them, to instill paranoia. Frausto's home was broken into twice. On both occasions, the intruders hacked into his computer and left the computer on to make it obvious they had been there (free speech organization Article 19 installed security cameras in his apartment). Later, he received an email, ostensibly from an airline, that contained the image of a ticket to Spain. Superimposed on it was the photo of one of his family members. The threat was clear. A cybersecurity expert confirmed it was the work of a hacker. On another occasion, when Frausto went to Huesca, Spain, to give a presentation, a young Black man approached him after the talk; Frausto had seen him back at the Mexico City airport before his flight. He warned Frausto that in Mexico they could kill not only little-known journalists, but high-profile journalists, too, just like in his own country, Togo. Meanwhile, Castellanos was also being followed, and by an albino man, lest she didn't notice.

With help from some of her colleagues, Castellanos tried to find a way to extricate her story from *El Universal* and take it to another media outlet. The paper's standard contract, which every contributor must sign, certainly didn't help: every writer must grant the paper all rights to their work, throughout the world and in perpetuity, with no additional remuneration beyond the initial payment. But an attorney with Article 19 found a way out: one clause stipulates that the granting of rights only takes effect once the work is published, not when it is submitted. And there was still another problem: Castellanos had made use of *El Universal* resources to carry out her investigation. Article 19 resolved this issue by providing money to reimburse the paper for expenses incurred and depositing the funds in one of the paper's bank accounts.

Now, Castellanos was free to try and find a media outlet to publish the piece, deal with any fallout from *El Universal*, and face the anger of the Mexican government. She turned to Carmen Aristegui and her news site, Aristegui Noticias.

On April 18, *El Universal* published an interview with Alfredo Castillo. He had not spoken publicly since he had been removed as "viceroy" of Michoacán, but even so the opportunity to ask him about the massacre in Apatzingán was ignored. After just a few weeks of unemployment after his dismissal, Castillo had rejoined the federal administration, now as general director of the National Commission for Physical Culture and Sport (CONADE). All he said in the interview was that his experience in the state "offered a different vision on how to bring athletics to the people, serving as an indirect way to prevent crime." The headline of the article was "I will make history leading CONADE."

That afternoon, the secretary of the interior issued a statement that he had received a video, delivered anonymously, that showed possible abuses of authority committed by the federal police in Apatzingán. A press conference was scheduled the following day.

The editorial team at Aristegui Noticias did not believe in coincidences. They thought the government would try to "burn the story": they expected a few facts on the massacre would be released in order to spin the story as much as possible. Again, this was damage control.

Castellanos and her colleagues devised a strategy to get their investigative report on the Apatzingán massacre to the public. To prevent any kind of preemptive strike and reprisals, Aristegui Noticias, *Proceso* magazine, and one foreign media outlet, the U.S. television network Univision formed an alliance of independent media. They would release the story simultaneously. Also, to combat any last-minute cyberattacks, they enlisted Article 19 to act as a mirror website.

On Sunday morning, with the hashtag #FueronLosFederales (#ItWasTheFeds), the story of how the federal police murdered unarmed civilians in Apatzingán went out around the world.[2] It was immediately picked up in Latin America, North America, and Europe.

Castellano's reconstruction of the events of January 6, 2015, in Apatzingán is based on recorded interviews of thirty-nine people she met in Apatzingán and in nearby towns, the contents of which have not been released in order to protect those interviewed. They were later verified, first by editors at *El Universal* and later by Aristegui Noticias, *Proceso*, and Univision. The interviewees included twelve of the forty-four detained and released in the first attack (including a shopkeeper), seven survivors of the second attack (three were hospitalized), a legal representative, eight witnesses, eight family members of victims, staff from Ramón Ponce hospital, and employees of the Forensic Medical Service (SEMEFO). Castellanos also made use of other relevant materials, including videos recorded by local residents and other audio recordings.

It turned out that Alfredo Castillo had recruited the crime syndicate Los Viagras, then a group of seven brothers who had deserted the Caballeros Templarios, to form a paramilitary group called Fuerza Rural (rural force). It was mainly comprised of laborers working the lime harvest, and their goal was to wipe out the Caballeros Templarios. For eight months, they pursued the leader, "La Tuta," through the mountains, but they were unable to capture him. When Castillo's failures and abuse of power became increasingly apparent to the public and his political adversaries used them against him, he ordered the demobilization of the Fuerza Rural. This did not go according to plan. He did not deliver the payments he had promised to the group, and their leader, El Gordo Coruco, decided to protest, directing the Rurales to hold a sit-in in front of the municipal palace in Apatzingán. After twenty days, Castillo ordered the protest crushed.

There had been two massacres that January 6. The first occurred around 2:30 a.m. There were still people out and about in the plaza because it was the eve of Three Kings' Day, or Epiphany—a day like Christmas, when Mexican children get up to open the presents they have been eagerly waiting for. Families mingled with the hundred or so protesters, some of whom were asleep in their cars while others were chatting in the park. On El Gordo Coruco's orders, they were unarmed, except for the six who would lay their firearms on the ground as soon as they were surrounded by the police. Some of the others had wooden sticks.

The police descended on them, some wearing black uniforms

and many with their faces covered. There was a shout of "Kill the dogs!" upon which they opened fire and the bloodbath began. It lasted all of fifteen minutes. Most people ran for cover. Surveillance footage showed people trying to escape. Those who followed the order to kneel and surrender were executed. Before he was detained, one of the Fuerza Rural who went by the name Artemio said he saw a policeman beating a woman who shouted at him that she was pregnant. The agent replied, "Shut up, bitch, or we'll kill you!" A witness reported that to cover up the death of Luis Alberto Lara, who was only twenty years old, the police officers ran over his body in their truck. That was apparently the hit-and-run Castillo referred to days later. Artemio noticed some families who happened to be in the plaza that night had been caught up in the violence. "We heard people crying, the women and children were hysterical." Out of the forty-four reported arrests, only twenty-five were members of the Fuerza Rural, according to El Gordo Coruco's people. Among the other nineteen were passersby, taxi drivers, bricklayers, and newspaper vendors. Eleven people who had been out shopping for toys that night were taken away in a truck, but they never turned up later in any prison. The exact number of deaths and injuries has never been confirmed.

Relatives and friends who lived on ranches and in small villages nearby listened to the victims' cries for help on radio transmissions and rushed to their aid. They were also unarmed so as "not to be treated like criminals," according to El Gordo Coruco. He did not want there to be any pretext for an armed attack from the police. At 7:20 a.m., they managed to locate a federal police convoy, and believing it was transporting their loved ones, a group got out of their truck and started smashing in the windows of a patrol car. The police responded by unleashing twenty minutes of gunfire from M60 machine guns, the kind used to penetrate armored cars. The civilians' vehicles were, of course, unarmored. A white pickup was in the line of fire, with seven youths ranging from sixteen to twenty years old inside. Four of them died. Behind them, in a black GMC Acadia was a man named Miguel Madrigal, with his family. Witnesses heard the women inside screaming that they were unarmed, pleading for the police to hold their fire. A horrific photo shows Madrigal and his wife on the ground trying to protect a young woman and a boy. They were all killed by high-caliber machine-gun fire that pierced their legs, torso, arms, skull. Among the few wounded who reached the hospital, an eighteen-year-old man had his pelvis, bladder, and rectum so seriously damaged that medics could easily touch his fragmented spine through the holes in his body. A seventeen-year-old received a failed coup de grâce; burned powder tattooed his open brain.

Interviews conducted by Castellanos discredit the assertions of Castillo that the federal police came to the aid of the wounded: what actually happened was they left them there to bleed to death. The police told paramedics there were no survivors, even though they could see movement among the bodies, and did not let them through. Later, the police prevented the transfers of some seriously wounded from town clinics to better-equipped hospitals, resulting in at least one death. Some bodies had been shot at point-blank range. No bodies were sent to the Apatzingán morgue. Castellanos found three death certificates of victims who had, inexplicably, been taken to cities three hours away. Photographs and videos indicated that the police had altered the positions of some of the bodies and planted weapons on them to make it look like the police had not initiated fire.

In a second installment, Castellanos revealed new documents and interviews confirming that not only the federal police had participated in the attacks but also the military. She had found that troops from the Thirtieth Infantry Battalion had fired on and detained people, and she reported that, of the forty-four arrested, the judge released forty-three for lack of evidence.[3] Later, Castellanos would present new evidence of the persecution of survivors and the family members of the victims, who have been detained, beaten, tortured, and forced to abandon their homes.[4]

Alfredo Castillo dismissed Castellanos's work as merely a collection of "anonymous statements," which could not have the same validity as testimonies of "people with first and last names." The attorney general of the republic, he said, "can, with no trouble and without violating the confidentiality of earlier findings, fully demonstrate the facts."[5] Castillo came up with his own media defense strategy, which was supported up by the journalists who were his allies. Carlos Marín, general editorial director of the powerful Grupo Milenio, coined the term "scavenger journalism" to define "the 'reconstruction' of the *Apatzingán executions*, based on *'recorded* interviews' of people with no identities," in what is nothing more than "the invention of journalistic tales."[6] This is one of the roles of Marín and his ilk: pleasing the powers they serve by discrediting journalists and anyone who contradicts them. On a television show a year later, discussing another massacre committed by federal police, this time of teachers in Nochixtlán, Oaxaca, Carlos Marín attempted to refute columnist Julio Hernández

"Astillero's" assertion that it was a crime of the state. Chuckling to emphasize how patently ridiculous the accusation was, he made a reference to the murder of Rubén Espinosa, Nadia Vera, and the three other women killed with them, saying, "They saw a state crime in the Narvarte crime just because some unknown photographer was in a brothel!"[7]

Nonetheless, Castellano's reporting was widely praised, garnering several awards, including the 2016 Latin American Investigative Journalism Award and the 2015 National Journalism Award. In her acceptance speech for the latter, Castellanos said, "That the federal police acted with complete impunity in this massacre, in view of local residents and passersby, was documented like no other that happened under Peña Nieto's administration. We had audio, video, photographic, and documentary evidence. But how many extrajudicial killings have we not covered because we don't know about them, or because there were no survivors?" She denounced censorship and the relentless attempts to discredit journalists: "There are professional editors and reporters at the paper," she acknowledged, but "I think the moment the management of *El Universal* decided not to publish my investigation on the massacre for two months, for political reasons, they became de facto accomplices of the perpetrators." In the audience was Francisco Santiago, editorial director of the paper.

She continued: "With this award, I hope the case of the Apatzingán massacre will gain new visibility. Because twenty-two months after the massacre, the attorney general of the Republic has not released its investigation. There has not been a single arrest. And the persecution of the survivors and their families continues. Thank you very much."[8]

8

Carmen Aristegui

"Angélica Rivera. At home with the first lady," read the cover of the May 2013 issue of *¡Hola!* magazine. "The first interview with the wife of the president of Mexico. In a historic exclusive, she invites us into her family's residence."

The mansion was located in Las Lomas de Chapultepec, one of Mexico City's wealthiest neighborhoods. From the photos in the magazine it looked impressive, its gleaming white walls, marble floors, and spacious bedrooms highlighting the mansion's luxurious elegance. Built to its future occupants' specifications, it was constructed on two adjacent plots of land, covering around 1,500 square meters, and its three stories, from its underground parking to its highest level, are connected by elevator. "Los Pinos will be on loan to us for six years," she told her children, referring to the official residence of the president in the nearby Bosque de Chapultepec, which every president has occupied during his term, since the 1930's and until Peña Nieto in 2018. "[The children's] real house, their home, is this one," she told the magazine.

Almost a year later, the website Aristegui Noticias, along with *Proceso* magazine, the daily *La Jornada*, and the website Sin Embargo, published a report by popular radio host Carmen Aristegui's special investigations unit called *La Casa Blanca de Peña Nieto* (The white house of Peña Nieto).[1] It transpired that the mansion that the First Lady had claimed to reporters was hers, that was guarded by the president's general staff and valued at $7 million, did not appear under Enrique Peña Nieto's or Rivera's name in the Public Registry of Property and Commerce. Instead, it was registered under Ingeniería Inmobiliaria del Centro, an affiliate of Grupo Higa, which is owned by the construction magnate Juan Armando Hinojosa Cantú.

In the fall of 2014, Peña Nieto's administration had opened the international bidding process for a construction project to build a high-speed railway between Mexico City and Querétaro, about 140 miles away. It was to be one of the signature projects of his term, and the contract was worth over $3.75 billion. Eighty-three companies had solicited bidding guidelines for the project, but only five had submitted bids. In fact, almost all of the companies, including the French company Alstom, the German Siemens, the Canadian Bombardier, and the Spanish CAF, had dropped out because they were not given sufficient time to prepare their proposals.[2] The only bidder that did not withdraw was a consortium comprised of the Chinese-government-owned China Railway Construction Company and the Mexican companies closely aligned with the highest echelons of power in Mexico.

Suspicions rose that this consortium received the required information ahead of everyone else. As was documented by the special investigations unit of Carmen Aristegui, host of a news show on MVS Radio, these suspicions proved right: Secretary of Finance and Public Credit Luis Videgaray had formed a "high-level working group" with the Chinese eleven months before the bidding process was announced.[3] On November 3, 2014, that consortium was awarded the contract.[4] Part of that consortium was Constructora Teya, an affiliate of the Higa Group owned by no other than Hinojosa Cantú, whose Ingeniería Inmobiliaria del Centro had registered the president's gleaming new home.

Peña Nieto and Hinojosa Cantú had a long-standing friendship, in which Hinojosa Cantú had received many lucrative contracts. When Peña Nieto was governor of Mexico State—which surrounds Mexico City and is the most populous state in the country—from 2005 to 2011, his administration awarded Hinojosa Cantú contracts worth over 30 billion pesos. Hinojosa Cantú had also contributed to Peña Nieto's presidential campaign: in 2012, another of Hinojosa Cantú's companies, Eolo Plus, managed transportation for Peña Nieto's campaign, charging around 26 million pesos. With his pal now president, things only improved: in less than two years, Grupo Higa had been awarded thirty-two federal contracts, directly or as part of the consortium that was awarded the contract to build the Monterrey VI aqueduct, a public works project valued at $3.6 billion.

The president's office knew about the "Casa Blanca" report before it was published. Reporters had asked them for an official statement, but instead of providing one, David López and Roberto Calleja, presidential staffers in charge of media management, maneuvered to bury the report. The president's transatlantic trip was extremely significant. In Beijing, aside from meeting with Chinese leadership, he would participate in the Asia-Pacific Economic Cooperation meeting, bringing together heads of state from Pacific Rim nations, the biggest trade region in the world.

Then he would continue on to Australia to attend the Group of 20 Summit. These were outstanding world-class platforms, where Peña Nieto wanted to dazzle as a young, visionary, reformist leader who was modernizing Mexico and driving the country forward. Given the recent news about the massacres at Tlatlaya and Iguala, he could not afford to have yet another scandal appear in the news.

The president's staffers soon realized that it would be impossible to stop the report, and Peña Nieto nullified the railway contract award three days before the article was to be published. His ostensible aim was "providing more transparency and clarity, so there are no doubts about the project."[5] The abrupt announcement surprised everyone, most of all the Chinese. Irate, they demanded $600 million in compensation.[6]

The first lady was also furious. On November 18, she released a seven-minute video in which she displayed profound displeasure with the journalists who had questioned their real estate holdings—and with everyone who had believed them. The house did not belong to the president, she claimed, but to her. She had told Hinojosa Cantú she wanted to buy a plot of land and build a house, and the construction magnate had offered to manage it for her, letting her pay him 54 million pesos over eight years, at a 9 percent interest rate. Rivera said she had already paid him 30 percent of the total.

"In light of all the accusations that have put my honor in doubt, I want to make it very clear to all of you, the Mexican people, that I have nothing to hide, I have worked all my life and thanks to that, I am an independent woman," she said. "I have been able to build a property honestly through all my hard work. I want to let you know I have decided to sell the rights derived from the buyer-seller contract, because I do not want this to continue to be a pretext to offend"—here she pauses for dramatic effect—"and slander my family. I am here today to defend my integrity, and my children's and my husband's. . . . I am not a public servant but I cannot allow this issue to call my honor into question, and above all to hurt my family."[7]

How could a soap opera actress come by not only that mansion, but other luxury residences, and an apartment in Miami? According to Rivera, she reached an agreement with the media group Televisa, where she had worked for decades, to compensate her for her services and also ensure she would not work for any other television network for five years. As a result, in 2010 she was paid 88 million pesos. "That is not normal," said another Televisa soap opera star, Kate del Castillo. "They never paid me like that. I never made that kind of money."[8]

The public did not find Rivera believable in her latest role either. The daily *Reforma* asked in a poll, "Do you believe Angélica Rivera's explanation of how she acquired the Casa Blanca?"; 77 percent of respondents said no, while only 13 percent said yes. And 66 percent thought Rivera had acted like an actress, just 19 percent like a first lady.[9]

The president himself made no apology. From his perspective, there was nothing wrong with the arrangement. In December 2014 he had tried to convince reporters of his innocence while talking with them informally on a flight, "What conflict of interest? I don't see one at all! Let's say I have a friend who is the owner of [telephone company] Nextel, and I buy a radio, or contract his company's services. Am I doing anything illegal? Am I favoring my friend? I don't think so. There is no conflict of interest just because I have a friend at Nextel and I chose this company and not another!"[10]

In February the following year, Peña Nieto named an old associate of his, Virgilio Andrade, as secretary of civil service. He was charged with investigating whether there had been any wrongdoing in the Casa Blanca case because, according to the president, "I am committed to strengthening legality and closing off possibilities of corruption." He went on to stress that "the president does not award contracts, or hand out projects, or participate in any service committee; I am aware that the accusations made inspired different opinions."[11]

Petite and slender, with short auburn hair, a fair complexion, and a big smile, Carmen Aristegui is one of the most popular radio hosts in Mexico. Her strength lies in the great warmth she exudes, her sense of justice, and the clear commitment she shows to the public and to journalism. This has given her the mettle she has needed when targeted as an enemy by the powers that be—an all-too-familiar occurrence in her career. A granddaughter of Republican refugees from the Spanish Civil War, she got her start in public TV network Imevisión in 1987, at the age of twenty-three, and her zealous embrace of independent journalism has led to many enemies in high places, eager to place obstacles in her way. In 2008 she was fired from W Radio, a property of Televisa and the Spanish corporation Grupo PRISA, allegedly at the behest of Juan Ignacio Zavala, brother of the wife of then president Felipe Calderón.

A year passed before Aristegui found a new home at MVS Radio, the new name for Stereorey, which had been founded by

Joaquín Vargas Gómez in 1967. Aristegui arrived at MVS, which was still owned by the Vargas family, in January 2009, but Calderón again called for her dismissal two years later for supposed ethics violations. A legislator in the Chamber of Deputies had accused the president of being an alcoholic, by then a common accusation leveled at Calderón. Reasoning that the president's health was a matter of public interest, Aristegui had said on the air: "We will leave the question open: does the president of the Republic have a drinking problem, or not?" She was accused of offending executive power without cause and was fired. Aristegui gave a press conference to denounce "the presidential temper tantrum, which she said "befitted a dictator." Her name trended on Twitter around the globe, and a large crowd of her followers staged a protest in front of MVS headquarters to demand her reinstatement. The radio network gave in.

A year later, in the final days of Calderón's administration, MVS president Joaquín Vargas revealed that the labor secretary, Javier Lozano, had threatened to revoke their license for the 2.5-gigahertz bandwidth: "If you rehire that journalist, your company will be ruined and you can forget about this government until its last day."

To Carmen Aristegui and her special investigations unit, made up of Irving Huerta, Rafael Cabrera, and Sebastián Barragán, and headed by Daniel Lizárraga, some form of retaliation for their Casa Blanca exposé was expected. Even so, they were caught by surprise four months later, on March 11, 2015, by an announcement during the commercial breaks in her news show—now the station's most profitable space. A recorded message stated that the network deemed it "egregious and offensive" that their company had been linked without its approval to MéxicoLeaks, a platform created in the mode of Wikileaks to help people securely share documents, especially anything concerning corrupt practices. It was immediately obvious that this was directed at Aristegui.

Aristegui maintained her own web portal, Artistegui Noticias, where she reproduced some of the items she presented every morning on her four-hour radio news show, Noticias MVS, on MVS Radio. In her contract with the radio network, the company guaranteed Aristegui editorial independence, and both parties signed a code of ethics that assured she and her colleagues enjoyed a certain level of autonomy.

Aristegui Noticias had joined MéxicoLeaks in the public interest, but according to MVS, this was unacceptable, and the next day it announced the dismissal of the reporters it identified as responsible—Lizárraga and Huerta. At the time, they were finishing up an investigation of finance secretary Videgaray, who apparently owned a luxurious vacation property in the town of Malinalco, which he had purchased under unusually favorable terms from the extremely generous and seemingly ubiquitous Hinojosa Cantú. "We knew it was a way to pressure Carmen, to force Carmen to resign," Lizárraga told me, "and we asked her not to."

MVS announced new rules for their news hosts that curbed their editorial independence. This violated the terms of MVS's contract with Aristegui, which was still in effect, but MVS refused to negotiate. Aristegui had, by this time, made it clear that she would only stay on as host if her colleagues who had been fired were reinstated. MVS responded by rejecting her ultimatum and firing her.[12] Despite being a financially painful move for MVS, the station decided to pull the plug on the show.[13]

After Arestigui was fired, hundreds of her supporters, including myself, gathered to protest in front of the MVS building. For two straight days, we chanted, "We are all Carmen!" and "You are not alone!" Reporters, artists, filmmakers, academics, students, business professionals, and laborers carried chayotes (a tropical vegetable symbolizing bribes for reporters), posters, and banners with handwritten slogans: "No to gag orders," "Another blow to democracy in Mexico," "MVS, Mexico condemns you," "Carmen: you were our voice for many years, now we will be yours!" and "Listening to Aristegui is an act of rebellion and hope." The cover of *Proceso* magazine featured a photo of the beleaguered journalist.

The story was covered by major international media, including the *Washington Post, The Guardian*, the BBC, and the leading outlets in Spain. "From a business perspective, the decision is difficult to understand," *Forbes* magazine reported.[14] According to the Associated Press, "The crusading host of Mexico's top-rated news radio program has been fired in a case that many fear is a blow to freedom of expression."[15]

Further protests followed. In just five days, the online petition #EnDefensaDeAristegui on change.org had been signed by 170,000 people (the slogan "MVS doesn't listen to over 170,000 people" was then projected onto the MVS building), and within a few weeks it would rise to 234,000 signatures.[16] "Staying silent is an act of complicity," wrote journalist Javier Valdez. México-Leaks also put out a statement: "The democratic values supported by this platform—among them freedom of expression, the right to information, transparency, and accountability—make this company [MVS] uncomfortable or could affect their interests," and rejecting the argument made by the radio broadcaster: "No commercial brand has been used for any aim beyond the work of journalism."[17]

Aristegui decided to hold a press conference. Its venue was to be the Memory and Tolerance Museum, in the center of Mexico City, but it was so overwhelmed by people that it had to be canceled. Hours later, Aristegui released a statement online: "Something very serious must have happened for the owners [of MVS], who are usually so attentive, to make them behave in this hostile and virulent way, trying to destroy journalists." She then compared what had happened with a pivotal event for independent journalism in Mexico: the gutting of the daily *Excélsior* by President Luis Echeverría in 1976. "This is nothing other than a coup," Aristegui said. "Mexico will not accept *echeverrista* practices. We urge MVS to not let the coup defeat them."[18]

In an interview published in *Proceso* the following weekend, Aristegui confirmed certain rumors that had been circulating: "All roads lead to the Casa Blanca," she said. The owners of MVS, the Vargas family, had tried to stop her report. "The situation between us was very tense and complex. Their tone wasn't dictatorial or imperious, but they were asking for my 'understanding.' In effect, their position was that if I reported this information on MVS News, it was understood that it would be the end of my show."[19]

MVS responded by saying that, contrary to their wishes, she had talked about the story constantly on air. They also said they had financed the investigation and accused Aristegui of syphoning company resources and redirecting them to her own web portal. This was despite the fact that it had been accepted practice for three years, from 2012 until 2015, and MVS would share in its social networks stories published on Aristegui Noticias. Aristegui also made it clear that she had done this to respect the wishes of MVS, which did not have to broadcast the report on their radio station. Aristegui had instead collaborated with *Proceso* and the daily *La Jornada* to publish it simultaneously with Aristegui Noticias. That was the reason why it became the biggest story of the week and was picked up by international media. The attention had, in turn, forced presidential spokesperson Eduardo Sánchez (who had acted as general counsel for MVS until a few months before) to make a statement saying the First Lady was buying the house as a personal purchase, without Peña Nieto's involvement, and she had the financial resources to do so.[20] This pressured all the media to acknowledge the fact, which allowed Aristegui to talk about it on MVS.

In spite of the support of her audience, she was the object of an intense smear campaign. She was accused of being arrogant, unreliable, manipulative, and a drunk, and she was pulled into an exhausting morass of lawsuits and countersuits. She worried for her staff. Twenty people had left MVS along with her: the four journalists of the investigative team, members of the production department, respected contributors, all of her foreign correspondents, even two young staffers in other departments who had been fired for expressing their opposition on private social media accounts. This act of reprisal was not an isolated incident but part of a pattern in which journalists who didn't toe the party line were silenced. In their annual report, "State of Censorship," Article 19 stated, "No matter the [federal] entity, censorship is applied with the goal of cutting off the voice of those who denounce a State that pretends to guarantee them human rights."[21]

In the middle of this national and personal firestorm, Aristegui was as calm and pleasant as she always was in gatherings with friends. She said her strategy was to continue demanding that she and her team be rehired through legal channels until that route was thoroughly exhausted.

After the street protests had died down, Aristegui's supporters had to figure out new way to take action. Initial ideas did not go beyond hashtag campaigns, and while #MexicoWantsAristegui-Back went viral, the government paid little attention. We had to find other ways to exert pressure. Some of Aristegui's friends, including me, started getting together at the home of journalist Blanche Petrich to discuss what we could do. We were the San Borja Group, named for the street in Colonia del Valle, Mexico City, where our host lived.[22]

We came up with the idea of launching a massive campaign to submit individual legal complaints from the public to the justice system, a tactic that as far as we knew had only been used once before in Mexico, in the city of Guadalajara when students opposed a transportation fare increase. We wanted to do this because, as Aristegui put it, "The audience has rights and they should demand them. This is a battle not just to defend a handful of journalists, but also to confront the regime's authoritarianism, acting against the freedoms and rights of journalists, audiences, and citizens."

We forged ahead with this plan, which carried with it significant logistical challenges. It was one thing to ask people to take two minutes to sign an online petition, and another to ask them to print out cumbersome forms, fill them out correctly, go to a courthouse with official identification to submit them, then wait for a response, and when requested, go back to ratify the terms of their legal claim. But if we succeeded, we might have our basic argument heard: under the current legal framework, MVS did not own the radio frequency it used; it was merely the license holder for this state-owned property, making MVS a representative of the state in matters relating to that property. If the state was obligated to guarantee the rights recognized by the Constitution, then that obligation would be transferred to the licensee acting in its name. As we understood it, MVS was legally obligated to protect the public's right to be freely informed from various sources, and it was only the public who could remove Aristegui.

Three lawsuits were filed against MVS: Aristegui's suit for breach of contract; another on behalf of academics Lorenzo Meyer, Denise Dresser, and Sergio Aguayo, who along with Aristegui were political commentators on the morning newscast and had reported workplace abuses; and another lawsuit on behalf of six civil society organizations (the National Association of Democratic Lawyers, ANAD; the National Center of Social Communication, CENCOS; Communication and Information of Women, CIMAC; Article 19 México; the Mexican Association for the Right to Information, AMEDI; and the Action Group for Human Rights and Social Justice, Grupo de Acción por los Derechos Humanos y la Justicia Social) for attacking freedom of expression.

So began one of the most inspiring stages of our resistance campaign. With a press conference, the launch of the website En Defensa de Aristegui (endefensadearistegui.wordpress.com), and an explanatory video, we invited people to legally challenge the firings of these journalists. The Rompeviento TV offices became the headquarters to receive the legal complaints from the public, filing them into hundreds of boxes. One of the staff told me, "A woman came in, a street vendor from far away, with her cooler of popsicles for sale, but first she wanted to stop by to fill out her complaint. She didn't know how to write, just her name. That kind of thing really moved me. And there was a blind person who asked for help filling out the forms. Women in wheelchairs, people with canes, there are so many, so many . . . and what they say: they want to build a better country, to do something, to fight so it can happen."

Using the hashtag #MiDerechoComoAudiencia (my right as the audience), we organized public events in different cities, with the organizers supplying the legal forms for people to fill out. Hundreds of people attended, lending their time to take part in this act of civic responsibility. We held the first in Mexico City at the Monument to the Revolution—it was inspiring to see so many people waiting in line, filling out the forms, asking questions, and expressing their support.

The San Borja Group directly collected and processed over 2,700 legal complaints.

Months later, Aristegui shared her excitement with me: "They say around four or five thousand people formally submitted legal complaints. That's amazing for us, but it's also a sign that a segment of the public is ready to fight." Yet that week she was unexpectedly prevented from attending an event in Coyoacán to greet her supporters, as we had planned.

The day before, on April 18, her website, Aristegui Noticias, had been disabled for twelve hours because of a two-pronged distributed denial of service (DDoS) cyberattack.[23] That morning, *El Universal* had published their interview with Alfredo Castillo, the former "viceroy" of Michoacán who had ordered the bloody intervention in Apatzingán (chapter 7). Later that same day, the secretary of the interior had issued a statement that a video had been delivered to him anonymously, showing possible abuses of authority committed by police in Apatzingán.

The little editorial team at Aristegui Noticias did not believe in coincidences. Rather they thought the government would try to "burn the story." They expected a few facts on the massacre would be released, in order to manipulate the story as much as possible in an attempt at damage control. Any investigative reports on the massacre would be buried by media outlets with the farthest reach, in TV, radio, digital, and print. In the best cases, there would be the odd short articles in back pages, destined to get lost in a sea of content. The massacre would only be given space when an official response from the authorities was published. The government had to have their say, especially where it was in service of discrediting any investigations that did not show it in a flattering light. Meanwhile, Aristegui Noticias would go on to publish the devastating report by Laura Castellanos, detailed in the previous chapter.

Beyond personality differences, media outlets in Mexico position themselves on opposite sides of a widening breach between outlets that follow the government line and those that engage in independent journalism and are willing to be critical of power. The censorship case against Aristegui and her team brought conflicts in the polarized Mexican press to the surface. Instead of showing professional solidarity, columnists such as Ricardo Alemán launched a barrage of invective against her. They viewed her as representing what they dismissively called "activist journalism," without acknowledging they themselves were engaged in activism by promoting PRI party causes. For instance: "With Peña Nieto, the most freedom of expression," ran the headline of Alemán's column in *Milenio Diario* a few weeks later on September 12, 2016. The president, he argued, is

> a democrat; all kinds of criticism are possible—even the most offensive and insulting—because unlike what went on in the past, today there is tolerance in the presidency, and no pressure, much less restrictions, is put on the media, companies, or even critics. As for the angry, vengeful, self-interested, militant voices, in today's Mexico we have complete freedom to criticize those in power, the president; to criticize the actions and decisions of the executive office, his policies, his associates, and his results. But the funny thing about this new virtuous phenomenon is that there is no shortage of idiots who confuse full freedom of expression and the tolerance of a democrat in the presidency, with the weakness of the government.[24]

This phenomenon was hardly new, especially for Aristegui. In just one example of many, Aristegui's team in March 2014 had embedded a reporter in the staff of Cuauhtémoc Gutiérrez, president of PRI in Mexico City and the boss of the "trash pickers," who dug through trash cans for reusable materials to sell and who had, in the past, acted as a goon squad for Gutiérrez. The Gutiérrez family flaunted their lavish wealth, which they made by exploiting the trash pickers who lived in abject poverty. Relying on videos, photos, audio recordings, and interviews, Aristegui's team was able to prove that the politician had used taxpayer money legally allocated for PRI campaign expenses to deceive, recruit, and pay young women seeking work in a prostitution ring to exclusively serve Gutiérrez.[25] Ciro Gómez Leyva, a radio host rivaling Aristegui for largest audience, invited Gutiérrez on his show several times to refute the accusations. Protected by his party's power, the PRI politician avoided any judicial prosecution, and on his show on Radio Fórmula, Gómez Leyva exploited this impunity to condemn Aristegui's report as "one of the most perverse, obscene cases of editorial abuse I have ever seen." In his column in *El Universal*, he reproached Aristegui and her team for "leaving without even apologizing to Cuahtémoc Gutiérrez."[26]

In Mexico, the pathways to justice greatly depend on who somebody is, and what resources and influence they bring to bear. Often, judges' decisions are not made independently of political and economic power. On April 16, one member of this new generation of judges, Fernando Silva, admitted an appeal filed by Aristegui, containing arguments that reflected our campaign's appeals: the court should issue a provisional ruling in Aristegui's favor because the radio company's actions had been based on the rights of a private entity, disregarding the fact that it concerned the "license of a public resource and service of the State" and ignoring the matter's social relevance, since in addition to Aristegui's rights, this was affecting journalistic practice and freedom of expression.[27]

"A precedent like this no doubt strengthens the autonomy of journalists, and strengthens guarantees in the face of corporate or state censorship," an analysis by Dr. José Roldán Xopa, professor at the Instituto Tecnológico Autónomo de México, said. "The decision will directly impact MVS, but it will be a precedent affecting all radio and television licensees; corporate power will be contained. In this environment," he concluded, "I would assume the licensee will evaluate their costs and benefits."[28]

But nothing came of it. MVS immediately rejected the decision and requested a different judge. Furthermore, the owners of the Mexican media using the state's electromagnetic spectrum sensed a potential threat to the control of their businesses, and through the National Chamber of the Radio and Television Industry, they asked to intervene in the dispute against Aristegui. If she forced MVS to reverse their firing, the ability of licensees to give and take away microphones and screens at their whim would be called into question.

For their part, surprisingly, the Peña Nieto administration assumed an active role in the legal process. Humberto Castillejos, legal advisor to the president, submitted an appeal in which he stated it was "inadmissible" and "absurd" to think licensees should have to consult their audiences to make programming decisions.

On July 14, a judicial tribunal friendly to the administration overturned the appeal filed by Aristegui. With that, she wrote, "They prevented Judge Silva from analyzing the allegations of the parties and resolving them judiciously." Therefore, "we did not lose the case, nor did they win, as a handful of self-appointed spokespeople have maliciously insisted. They killed the case by simply presenting a complaint [from the trade group]. It will be hard for other journalists to seek justice for acts of censorship against freedom of expression."[29]

The thousands of official complaints filed by employees, colleagues and listeners were cast aside.

In the meantime, Secretary of Civil Service Virgilio Andrade continued with his investigation into the Casa Blanca scandal, presenting his conclusions later in 2015. They came as no surprise. He confirmed that Angélica Rivera had the financial resources to purchase the house; that after the scandal, she had canceled the buyer's contract; that Grupo Higa had refunded payments she had already made; and that she gave them 10.5 million pesos as compensation. He also found the president was not responsible for awarding contracts and exercised no influence over the thirty-three contracts the federal government had granted to subsidiaries of Grupo Higa during his term.[30]

Reporters noted that Andrade had not questioned Rivera or Hinojosa Cantú or the president himself. He had not investigated Peña Nieto's term as governor of Mexico State, when Grupo Higa had prospered in his shadow; nor had he looked into the mysterious process of awarding and then canceling the contract for the train to Querétaro.

Almost a year later, the government still could not shake off the scandal. At that point Peña Nieto came forward to admit what he called a mistake:

> Public servants, aside from having a responsibility to act according to the law with complete integrity, are also responsible for the perceptions our actions create.

And in that I admit I made a mistake. Even though I acted according to the law, this error affected my family, hurt the beginning of the administration, and weakened the public's trust in the government. I myself felt the Mexican people's irritation. I understand it perfectly. So, I very humbly ask for forgiveness, and repeat my most sincere apology for the aggravation and indignation that I caused.[31]

This gesture "has historic implications," columnist Ricardo Alemán stated, "because the president not only accepts a political error—the Casa Blanca—but also provides a solution: the National Anticorruption System." We should "recognize the gesture," Héctor Aguilar Camín suggested.

"That was it," Aristegui responded in a seven-minute video. "In any other country, with real rule of law, an independent investigation would have been conducted, an impeachment or judicial proceeding, and very likely the president would have been forced to resign. Not in Mexico. In Mexico, the president is still in office, and we journalists who worked on the Casa Blanca investigation, and encouraged the debate on its serious implications, were thrown off the air on Mexican radio. We won't be back on the air . . . at least, not until after this six-year term is over."[32]

It took the San Borja Group a year to convince Aristegui to find an alternative outlet for her show online, outside of radio, where she would certainly not be allowed to return as long as Peña Nieto was in office. Aristegui Noticias still operated, trying to keep together the team that MVS had fired in March 2015, but the live news broadcast was not relaunched on its website because the expenses required for offices, equipment, salaries, and production costs were prohibitively high. Even though we thought Carmen's popularity would allow her to meet those expenses—her show on MVS had been the station's main source of ad revenue—she worried about being at the mercy of financial concerns. She didn't want to have to sell ad space only to be pressured into sacrificing her editorial independence.

But on March 15, 2016, she decided to go ahead and resume broadcasting live. Not only did she have to deal with the numerous business and technical challenges that entailed, but the harassment intensified once she made the announcement. In Mexico, the offensive on social media had begun: influencers such as @callodehacha, a YouTuber who reportedly received at least 47 million pesos—$2.5 million—in advertising from Peña Nieto's administration,[33] and bots circulated false information on social media, linking Aristegui to certain business moguls and posting death threats. They accused her of being a puppet of Mexican tycoon Carlos Slim.[34] On November 13, five men entered the building where Aristegui Noticias was headquartered, restrained the security guard, broke into Aristegui Noticias's offices, and stole a computer. In a show of impunity, the burglars looked directly at the nine security cameras, their faces uncovered, showing no concern. Even so, the police didn't manage to identify them.[35] (With the same disregard for being identified, three men ransacked *Proceso*'s offices a year later, on May 21, 2017, for unknown reasons.[36])

MVS, meanwhile, had gone from criticizing the alleged use of their brand on MéxicoLeaks to accusing Aristegui of refusing to follow the company's new editorial guidelines, and of misappropriating company resources. They filed a lawsuit against her and the publisher of *La casa blanca de Peña Nieto* by Daniel Lizárraga and his colleagues in the special investigations unit, for which Carmen had written a foreword.

In her foreword, Aristegui lamented "the moral failing of Joaquín Vargas and his brothers [the owners of MVS], who I had truly admired very much," since "it was tragic to see how they, who had invested in freedom of expression and journalistic investigation, in the end succumbed to pressures and shady dealings of a power who they had confronted bravely and with dignity before."[37] MVS demanded the foreword be cut.

On November 14, as she accepted the Knight International Journalism Award, presented by the International Center for Journalists (ICFJ) in Washington, DC, she said: "Before arriving in Washington, I got word of the first judgment against me in one of several cases brought by the same powers who censored us and threw us out of Mexican radio. A judge charged me with 'excessive use of freedom of expression and of information' for what I wrote in the prologue to the book *La casa blanca de Peña Nieto*."[38]

The lawyers for MVS claimed that Aristegui did not give any evidence to show that the Vargas brothers "succumbed to pressures and shady dealings," and therefore, they maintained, this was defamation. They sued Aristegui for unspecified damages—possibly in the millions of pesos. As for the publisher, Penguin Random House Mexico, MVS only demanded an apology and the omission of the foreword in future printings of the book. "They are trying to separate the publisher from the author, and we do not agree with this separation," responded editorial director Ricardo

Cayuela. "We will publish the foreword because it meets the highest standards of journalism."

In Washington, Aristegui concluded her speech: "For Mexico to escape from this profound crisis in human rights and political rot, we must speak out in a loud voice, report widely, provide oxygen for the public debate, and shake Mexican society. We must have free and independent journalism. . . . In this time of efforts to hide the truth, of authoritarian backsliding, of intolerance and incitement to hate—in this time of Donald Trump—let us celebrate journalism and defend our freedoms."[39]

On January 16, 2017, twenty-two months after getting pushed out of MVS, the news program *Aristegui en Vivo* (Aristegui live) began broadcasting online on the internet, following a brief promotional ad campaign. Its tag line? "Did they really think they could shut us up?"

In February 2019, Aristegui won the two lawsuits against MVS after four years of litigation: in separate decisions, the Supreme Court ruled that the company's breach of their contract with her was "illegal and without cause," and they overturned the ruling against her for nonmaterial damages. The Casa Blanca investigation, meanwhile, had been recognized for the incredible piece of journalism that it was. It was awarded a National Journalism Award and a Gabriel García Márquez Journalism Award, the most prestigious Spanish-language award.

9

Javier Valdez

The outside temperature had climbed to 104 degrees. About fifteen miles from the town of Los Mochis, in the state of Sinaloa, three state police officers did not dare venture outside the airconditioned comfort of their truck. From its cool interior, they watched Mirna Nereyda Medina Quiñones and others in the group they had been assigned to protect as they toiled in the dirt, the salty earth reflecting the sun's heat. They pierced holes in the ground with a rod to see if it came up smelling of death, then dug into the earth with a shovel, turning over the dirt, sweat dripping down their faces like tears.

Mirna Nereyda's son, Roberto, had been abducted from the gas station where he worked selling auto parts in the nearby town of El Fuerte on July 14, 2014. Witnesses reported he was taken away by municipal police officers in a black Explorer. Mirna had been looking for him ever since. To Mirna, the authorities could not be trusted. They were negligent and probably complicit in what had happened to her son. She decided to act on her own. She gathered together other men and women whose loved ones had vanished, and formed *Las Rastreadoras*, the Trackers. On Wednesdays and Sundays, they went searching in and around the towns of north Sinaloa, along the Pacific Coast, for their loved ones. The first week, they went to the outskirts of the town of Los Mochis, the next near Guasave, the next near El Fuerte. Then they would return to Los Mochis and start again.

On this day, near Los Mochis, there were twenty-five people—nineteen women and six men. That was more men than usual. "Lately, since they have become more aware of what is going on, they say, well, I'm going to help, too," Mirna said. "The shovels can be very heavy for us, the picks, the machetes, but the women also work really hard."

Understandably, each person in the group wanted to go to the site where they believed their own loved one might be buried, and it upset some that they couldn't. But this day was different. They had heard that three days earlier three to five bodies had been buried on public land in Bachomobampo, near Los Mochis, about a hundred yards away from the nearest houses. Because they had been buried so recently, the bodies would presumably still be in relatively good shape.

There are graves all across Mexico. In a 2018 investigative report, "The Country of 2,000 Clandestine Graves," a twenty-member team of journalists documented the discoveries of 1,978 clandestine graves in twenty-four states, which had been dug between 2006 and 2016.[1] These graves contained at least 2,884 bodies, 324 skulls, and thousands of other bones and bone fragments. Only 1,738 victims had been identified by the time the report was published. They included men and women, the young and the elderly, even infants still dressed in baby clothes. The five states with the highest number of graves were Veracruz with 332, Tamaulipas with 280, Guerrero with 216, Chihuahua with 194, and Sinaloa with 139.

There are groups like the Trackers all over Mexico. I've accompanied similar search parties in the hills of Iguala, Guerrero, and in the Mexicali desert and in Tijuana, Baja California. All the sites were all on dry land, which made the work relatively easier. But in Bachomobampo, it had rained heavily by the time the Trackers arrived at the graves, and the area was flooded. The brother-in-law of one of the disappeared slogged through waist-high water. It was futile—they would have to wait until the water drained away. The group relocated to a different site on firmer, drier land. Fortunately, it wasn't nearly as hot there.

The T-shaped rod they used to pierce the earth was almost four feet long, and I watched them pushing down on it with all of their weight. "When you pull it out, you bring the tip to your nose, and if you detect a smell, that means there's something there," Mirna told me. "We almost don't like to use the rod because it damages the bodies." The bodies need to be shown the respect they deserved, she said. "People call them bones, skeletons. We call them treasures. We're not looking for bones, we're looking for treasures."

The Trackers believed that fifteen to twenty individuals had been buried in the area, and they found signs suggesting more were on their way. A large hole had been dug with what looked a piece of machinery, "as if they had it all ready to use," Myrna said. "We're watching it to not let it happen. Or if they get one over on us, we will come as soon as possible and remove the bodies immediately."

Yesenia, one of the founders of the Trackers, said they had been harassed several times by armed men, who had on occasion fired over their heads. "They're terrifying!" she said, grimacing. Despite her height and her imposing build, Mirna admitted she was scared, too. In the past, the group had been forced to leave some sites, "but we come back, because we're very stubborn."

Javier Valdez, a journalist at the local weekly paper *Ríodoce*, had been one of the first journalists to cover the group's work. "Javier was like my Jiminy Cricket," Mirna told me. She told him everything she was going to do. In his book, *Huérfanos del narco*, he described Mirna:

> A few months ago, in the first half of 2014, she thought that all the talk about people disappearing was an issue far removed, off in the distance, it didn't even touch her peaceful life, which was full of certainty, in spite of the financial ups and downs. She saw it in the papers over and over and heard on the radio about the sit-ins, the marches, family members' protests, in Sinaloa and the rest of the country. But like so many people who would rather not know about the tragedy, Mirna wanted to feel beyond its reach: 'Thank God I have my sons. My two sons. Young men, healthy. All this about disappearances, kidnappings, and executions, that won't happen to me.' Here she is now, out in the scrubland and the mountains, searching the horizon for a sign of hope, digging under the clouds to find the remains of her son Roberto.

According to Mirna, Javier approached her one day and said, "Listen Mirna, how do you do it, how do you go about your search?"

She told him that she would walk "along the banks of the river, along canals, pathways, highways."

"You're tracking," he said.

"Yes, I'm tracking."

"So from now on you'll be called a tracker. Your group will be called the Trackers." Javier and his *Ríodoce* colleague Luis Fernando Nájera named the group *Las Rastreadoras*. In his stories, he denounced the main suspects—Jesús Carrasco Ruiz, subdirector of the state ministerial police, and Santos Mejía Galaviz, ex-commander of the municipal police in El Fuerte—blaming them for the many disappearances in the area, among other crimes.[2] But what the Trackers had appreciated most was that Javier was interested in them as people. He was clearly interested in their loved ones—their sons, their husbands, their brothers, their friends who had disappeared. He knew that they deserved to be understood. As the Trackers rightfully said, you should not talk about violence without getting to know the individuals it impacts.

"I have always preferred to give a face and a name to the victims," Javier said when he accepted the International Press Freedom Award from the Committee to Protect Journalists in 2011, "to create a portrait of this sad and desolate panorama, these leaps and bounds and shortcuts toward the Apocalypse, instead of counting deaths and reducing them to statistics."

At the time of the award, Javier was forty-four years old. He had been a reporter for twenty-one years. Eight years earlier, in 2003, he had founded the weekly *Ríodoce* along with Ismael Bojórquez,

Andrés Villarreal, and others who had left the main Sinaloan daily, *Noroeste*, around the same time. Why the name *Ríodoce*? Its headquarters were located in Culiacán, the capital of Sinaloa, a state with eleven *ríos*, or rivers. Their publication would be *doce*, number twelve, and it would be a river, a conduit, of information. Its mission was to focus on major local issues, mainly consisting of investigative reporting "from a critical perspective." It had been deliberately founded as a counterweight to the "strong control of the media by the state government" and "the fratricidal war provoked by the drug cartels." Unsurprisingly, the governor of Sinaloa, Juan Millán, wasn't entirely pleased with them. "We're going to starve them to death," he said.[3] But he failed.

Through *Ríodoce*, Javier grew as an investigative journalist, developing a significant readership for his column Malayerba (bad weed). "Roll it up and smoke it," he said, when he introduced it on Twitter. He set up office in a restaurant called El Guayabo, a hundred yards from *Ríodoce's* actual office, where he could usually be found at the table by the front door. There was even a place in the restaurant for his trademark panama hat. El Guayabo had the nostalgic feel of a cantina. Roast chicken was the house specialty, but the *aguachiles*, full of shrimp and drenched in strong *chiltepín* peppers, made you shiver with pleasure. It was also a place for the local community to gather. A collection of colorful personalities, Javier's friends, set the mood. There was Casimira, the peanut vendor, and El Zurdo, "Lefty," who had dressed in all white ever since he started waiting tables there forty-one-and-a-half years ago—"in March," he added, wanting to be precise.

Javier was always a warm and friendly presence there. He was a great fan of rock and jazz, known for jamming on the drums at parties or local bars, and his writing was rich in metaphor and poetic turns of phrase. He wrote with the bitterness of someone with only a glimmer of hope that the lives of the people he wrote about—the children, women, and young people devastated by the day-to-day violence—would change for the better. But he also believed that glimmer was better than no hope at all. It would be a long road, but someone had to start somewhere, and he would start by telling stories.

In his book *Con una granada en la boca* (With a grenade in the mouth)—one of a number he would publish—he wrote:

> I gather a series of testimonies on human beings who have no more tears to cry and, even in the most miserable of conditions, dig the dry land to find their missing ones. Men and women who don't dream anymore, they don't sleep, for their life is an everyday nightmare; many left their houses, others never had one, for some homes are a joke, and only night and its mysteries give them comfort to voice their pain and how fucked they are."

At the Eduardo Galeano forum at Mexico City's Zócalo book fair in 2015, wearing his trademark panama hat, dressed in black, and perched on a chair that was clearly too small for him, he spoke about his book *Huérfanos del narco*. The book was about the children orphaned by violence caused by crime syndicates operating in Sinaloa. He was talking about how challenging it had been to interview the children, to get them to share their stories: "None of them, none of these kids who saw a parent die, who were with them in the car, in their own driveways, or waiting for the parents to come back, none of them suggested revenge, not one. They all hoped their parents would return. This exercise in hope, their pure, noble, honest, optimistic, tender, loving stories are what helped me grow as a reporter, and as a human being."

Sinaloa has changed considerably over the decades. Fifty years ago, marijuana production had operated on a relatively small scale, but from the 1980s, when Javier was a young man, larger-scale enterprises took over, with the support of PRI governor Leopoldo Sánchez Celis. In the hands of his son's godfather, Miguel Ángel Félix Gallardo, and his associates, and under the protection of the Federal Security Directorate, marijuana grew into an international operation. Many of those responsible for its growth wound up in prison, leaving their deputies to fight among themselves for control. Juan José "El Azul" Esparragoza, Ismael "El Mayo" Zambada, and Joaquín "El Chapo" Guzmán came out on top to lead the Sinaloa Federation, or the Sinaloa Cartel, as it was later dubbed by the authorities and media. It became the largest supplier of drugs to the U.S. market.

As a result, the ties among politicians, organized crime, and the police grew ever tighter as they consolidated power, and the general populace lost out. Protests were crushed and dissent silenced. Social activists and political rivals disappeared, or were jailed and killed. Their land was taken away, as happened to presidential candidate Manuel Clouthier in 1988; the following year, he was killed by a heavy truck on a Culiacán highway, an accident many feel was orchestrated. It was a reign of terror. By the second decade of the twenty-first century, the situation had deteriorated even further.

There were 397 homicides in 2007. By 2010, the number spiked to 2,397. It has since dipped but was on the rise again with 1,611 in 2017.

Life was especially dangerous for journalists. Ismael Bojórquez, the director of *Ríodoce*, says the turning point for local journalism came in 2004 and 2005, when reporters Gregorio Rodríguez and Alfredo Jiménez Mota were murdered. They were followed by José Luis Romero in 2009, Humberto Millán in 2011, and Atilano Román and Antonio Gamboa in 2014. "The most important newspaper publishers in Sinaloa instructed their reporters not to write a single article that did not corroborate official data," he said. "That is: stop doing any investigative work. Since 2005, in Sinaloa, there has been no journalism about narco-trafficking. When a subject touches on a narco, it stops right there."

Javier continued reporting. He didn't believe in apathy. He believed that he was making a valuable contribution. "I would rather do the work I should do as a journalist instead of playing the fool and looking the other way," he said at the Zócalo book fair event. "I see that a good portion of journalism in this country is kissing the ass of the powerful, and amplifying their rhetoric— of the governor, the mayor, the head of the government, and the president. I believe in doing my work. It's not a choice, it's my responsibility."

A woman in the audience asked if the reporting took a toll on him.

"I can't deny I have health problems," he said. "I have insomnia, and, yes, I cry a lot. I think crying helps me, when I hear these stories it makes me very sad, and when I write about them, too. I dance by myself, because I'm a terrible dancer, and that helps.

I make a fool of myself, but in private. I have my tequilas. I go to therapy. I manage not to make myself sick worrying about whether they're following me, if I can go out or not. I know when they decide, they can shoot you because they're in charge. In Mexico, we're used to violence," because "we see it so often it doesn't scare us, we don't want to see because we don't want to suffer, because suffering is being involved, and we don't want to get involved."

Doña María Herrera was in the audience that day. She was the mother of four sons who had disappeared. Short in stature, with a dark complexion and graying hair, she was the epitome of tenacity, of persistence, in a nation filled with people searching for their missing loved ones. "I ask myself," she said to Javier, "they have murdered, they have assassinated, they have silenced so many journalists. And the public? We carry on like it's nothing. As long as this keeps happening, we're never going to find our children. We need all those journalists who stay quiet, who are scared for their lives, to speak out."

In early 2017, Javier received a call from a stranger, asking for a meeting. The man claimed he represented Los Chapitos, the sons of "El Chapo," arguably the most notorious crime boss in Mexico.

Guzmán's origins were humble. He was born in 1957 to a family of farmers in Badiraguato. Like most families in the area, his worked in the poppy fields to produce opium gum. At the time, the market for poppies lay in the north, in the United States.[4] Like his father, Guzmán started as a *gomero* cultivating poppies, but at fifteen, he switched to marijuana production. He soon became involved in organized crime, rising through the ranks by working first for Héctor "El Güero" Palma, then the Sinaloa Cartel's founder and head, Miguel Ángel Félix Gallardo. With his skill in international transport logistics, he consistently made himself a valuable asset. When his *patrón* was arrested in 1989, he swiftly positioned himself at the top, the same level as other drug lords. El Chapo, which means "Shorty" because of his short stature, was a ruthless man. He was known for the violence, speed, and deadliness of his retribution when it came to anyone he thought had failed or betrayed him. Although he fantasized about the lifestyle of the people he saw in Mexican telenovelas and Hollywood movies, he lived a relatively austere lifestyle. He did have a weakness for beautiful women, which proved useful in tracking him. In 2012, in Los Cabos, El Chapo narrowly escaped being captured by police at a house where he was staying with a sex worker; he left only five minutes before police arrived. When El Chapo was finally captured in 2014, he was in bed with his wife in a house in Mazatlán.

El Chapo escaped prison twice, first by hiding in a laundry car in 2001, and then through a mile-long tunnel in 2015. Dámaso López, then deputy director of the Puente Grande maximum-security jail, helped with El Chapo's 2001 prison escape. In exchange for considerable sums of money, a home, and medical care for one of his children, López provided El Chapo with a cell phone, clothing, and secret visits. As a result, he went from being a prison official to a trusted member of the crime boss's inner circle.

When El Chapo was caught and jailed for the third time on January 8, 2016, he was extradited to the United States, where he was charged on ten counts of continued criminal enterprise, drug trafficking, and conspiracy.

A war of succession broke out between Dámaso López and El

Chapo's sons Jesús Alfredo and Iván Archivaldo Guzmán—Los Chapitos. In August 2016, both Guzmán brothers were abducted at the beach resort of Puerto Vallarta by the Cártel de Jalisco Nueva Generación, which had been expanding into the Sinaloa Cartel's turf. Thanks to the mediation of "El Mayo" Zambada, their father's partner, they were released five days later. Even though CJNG was known to be responsible, in a letter to radio presenter Ciro Gómez, Los Chapitos accused Dámaso López of having plotted the abduction.

This is where Javier steps in. Hoping to make amends, López had a representative contact Javier for an interview.[5] Javier, against his better instincts, agreed. In the meeting, the representative assured Javier that López had nothing to do with the abduction and that he "could not be the enemy of the sons of someone he loves and respects." The envoy insisted, "Everything can be resolved with a nice talk."

The brothers were in no mood to talk. They refused to even hear López's proposal. Bojórquez told me that Los Chapitos had their intermediaries ask them "not to publish the interview. We said no. They asked if they could buy out the print run of the paper. We said no. They asked us not to distribute the issue, we said no." Javier's story was published in the February 20, 2017, issue of *Ríodoce*. "Then they had to go to every store, follow around the distributors to five hundred, six hundred stores throughout the entire state, and everywhere they went, they bought all the papers," said Bojórquez. In any case, "we published the story online, on our website."

Ríodoce was not unfamiliar with threats from organized crime groups. In 2009, someone broke into the weekly's offices in the early hours of the morning and threw a grenade under an old heavy-built metal desk. The grenade exploded but didn't cause much damage. No one claimed the attack. "When you wake so many vipers, you never know which one will bite you," Bojórquez told me.

After Javier's interview with López, tensions mounted. At the paper, they decided Javier should leave Culiacán for a while. They reached out to their friend Carlos Lauría, the Americas program coordinator for the Committee to Protect Journalists (CPJ), who proposed that he leave the country. Weeks passed without a final decision being made. On April 14, Javier went out with his wife, Griselda Triana; their children, Tania and Francisco; and some friends to celebrate his birthday. He played the drums and wore a T-shirt that read, "Life Begins at 50."

Despite the celebrations, his heart was heavy. A few weeks earlier, on March 23, 2017, in Chihuahua City, Miroslava Breach was in her car, waiting for her fourteen-year-old son so she could take him to school. Fifty-three-year-old Miroslava was a correspondent for *La Jornada* and the founder of the Red Libre Periodismo (Free journalism network). She was a tough, dedicated, and intrepid reporter. "You could find her up in the mountains, going to places where many reporters had never been, even where the police wouldn't go," her colleague Rolando Nájera told me. She wrote about the murder of women in Ciudad Juárez, women looking for their daughters, the destruction of the environment, the violence suffered by the indigenous Tarahumara communities, and the ubiquitous political corruption. She investigated the relationship between members of the PAN and PRI parties with organized crime, which often supported candidates for office and financed their campaigns. "She was a journalist who made a lot of people uncomfortable," Nájera said, "not just organized crime groups, but the government, and crooked businessmen."

Clearly in someone's eye, she went too far and needed to be silenced. The morning of March 23, someone walked up to the window of her car and, with the quick, steady hand of an experienced assassin, fired eight shots from a 9-millimeter weapon.

Though the investigation advanced slowly, an overview of the crime gradually took shape. Miroslava had discovered that Los Salazar, a division of Gente Nueva, which in turn was an armed wing of the Sinaloa Federation, had appointed one of their own, Juan Salazar, to be the PRI candidate for mayor of Chínipas.[6] But because of her coverage, they were forced to replace Salazar with another candidate. After that, Miroslava's days were numbered.

Miroslava's death hit Javier especially hard. She had been a close friend, and it had already been an especially brutal month for journalism in Mexico, with two other reporters killed in Veracruz and attempts made on the lives of at least three others. Even the press aligned with power was starting to feel the heat: the deputy director of *Nexos* magazine, Héctor de Mauleón, received a series of death threats on Twitter, similar to threats sent to many other journalists, myself included.

With all the fury and bitterness that made his writing so powerful, Javier tweeted, "They killed Miroslava for speaking out. They can kill us all, if the death penalty is the sentence for reporting on this hell. No silence."[7]

Protests were held across Mexico. "You can't kill the truth killing journalists!" we chanted at protests in every corner of Mexico. At a demonstration held on the steps of the cathedral in

Culiacán, journalists placed microphones, recorders, cameras, and video cameras alongside three votive candles bearing the names of Miroslava and two other journalists who had been killed. Javier had been chosen to read the text that the protests' organizers had agreed should be read at all of the demonstrations:

> We do not demand special treatment. Only the constitutional guarantees to continue doing journalism and exercising our freedom of expression without our physical, psychological, and emotional integrity being destroyed by this vengeful violence, because the stories we tell make some uncomfortable, because they don't suit those with actual and constitutional power to have the truth get out. 99.5 percent of cases [of aggressions] have not been brought to justice, which in this country has become a metaphor of evasion.

"Javier saw himself in Miroslava," Bojórquez told me. "That's why he posted that tweet: 'They can kill us all.'"

On Monday, May 15, a little over month after Javier's fiftieth birthday, Bojórquez left the *Ríodoce* office to go to the bank. The editors had just ended their morning meeting. Javier had called his wife, Griselda Triana, to confirm he was having lunch with his son, Francisco. After finishing up at the bank, Bojórquez headed back to the paper's office. At the intersection of Riva Palacio and General Iturbe streets, two blocks from his destination, he saw a body lying in the middle of the road. At first, he thought someone might have been hit by car, a middle-aged man, by the looks of it.

Then he spotted the panama hat. And the boots. He rushed over. Two young people confirmed it had been no accident. "They just offed him," they told him. Bojórquez "walked around the body to see the face. It was Javier."

Two young men had apparently forced him out of his car and fired twelve shots at him, right in the middle of the day.

Later, Griselda recalled those horrible moments after she learned of his death. We spoke in her living room, sitting next to photos of her husband and underneath a black-and-white oil painting of Carlos Santana, a musician Javier admired. Bojórquez had called her to let her know about the attack. "I said that can't be, it can't be, I just talked to him. How is he? And then Ismael started crying. I said tell me how he is. And he just kept crying. Then I hung up the phone." She got to the scene of the shooting minutes later. The police let her through. His body was face down on the pavement, gun shells scattered around. His head was resting on his panama hat.

In the middle of all the grief and anger, we again held protests—at the Angel of Independence, in front of the National Palace, at the federal attorney general's office, at state offices, all the now tragically familiar places. Where had we not been? Where could we go to make sure our voices were heard? What good would it do?

We went to the Secretariat for Home Affairs. We projected photos of Javier and of his work onto the building. We projected the video of his speech accepting the International Press Freedom Award in New York. A group of residents from the Los Pedregales area in Coyoacán arrived, led by Fili, an elderly indigenous woman with a strong, defiant bearing. When we first met, in her neighborhood built on volcanic rock, where she had led the struggle for indigenous rights for fifty years, she gave me a gift. It was a rock wrapped up in a handkerchief. "We give rocks to our friends," she had said. "We throw them at our enemies." Now she said, "We must cry out for justice, yes, but we know that we're not going to get it from them—the government." Her group carried posters with Javier's image. Torches were lit. They looked beautiful in the flickering light in the encroaching darkness.

Demonstrators remembered the fallen journalists. They recited their names. The list seemed to go on forever. Javier was now the 105th journalist to be killed this century, according to the tally by free speech organization Article 19—the 32nd in Enrique Peña Nieto's term alone. A huge Mexican flag, its red and green replaced with black and the eagle of the national coat of arms inverted, was draped over the entrance to the complex, serving as a backdrop for the speakers. "These are not isolated incidents," warned a sign placed on the ground by Amnesty International volunteers, amid votive candles and photos of Miroslava and Javier. It was growing difficult to hold back the tears. Some didn't even try. A number of journalists who had been forced to leave their homes and seek refuge in the capital spoke before the crowd. People who had been affected by violent crime spoke up. "You can't kill the truth killing journalists!" the crowd chanted.

Doña María Herrera—the woman who was searching for four disappeared sons and who had spoken up at the Zócalo book fair—came forward to say, "The blood Javier shed is a stain on all of us. [Javier] was a human being who was at our side through the pain and suffering. He understood a hundred percent the battle we have waged for years to find peace, and justice. And with great pain, sadness, and indignation, we see that was not enough to respect his life, and in taking him, they have taken a part of ourselves. We are not afraid, we will not be intimidated."

"These are Javier's words," began journalist Lydia Cacho, as she read an excerpt from one of his books:

> One may also wonder, why write at all, why go out and get the story, risk your life, if we all have family, children, parents, if we have, even if it's only remnants, illusions, hope, why the hell go out into the terror, to see the bodies on the highways, hands tied, with their brains blown out, why report on the protest, if the powers from on high ordered the riot police to go after the photographer, the reporter, after that young woman reporter, "fuck her up," why get home at midnight to stand watch, to try and find out where that missing student is, that teacher, that worker, that migrant, or someday your brother, your girlfriend, your daughter, our own blood. But you still do it, go out into the horror, have a beer under the grumbling sun, take the offensive photo and go ahead with the report, cling to a thread of hope to create a little awareness, a touch of sensitivity, in the eyes and in the soul. Write a story, rush to file it, tell the truth, even if we're afraid, name names, the time and place, the motive, report from the abyss, have a voice, just loud enough to tell the reader this, too, is real life.[8]

Carmen Aristegui also spoke: "Javier Valdez and all the others who have lost their lives on this road should serve to motivate us." She took up Javier's call to action: "No silence. No self-censorship. No fear. Here, together, we have to give one another the courage to go on reporting. To keep on getting the story, keep on informing, keep on raising our voice, speak up, speak up, speak up."

"No silence!" we chanted in unison, "No silence! No silence!"

Mirna Nereyda knew she was in danger. Her defiance had prompted a steady stream of death threats demanding that she stop exhuming the dead. Javier had warned her several times. She had finally found her "treasure"—on July 14, 2017. No one had suggested that her son, who had disappeared three years earlier, might be buried there. But she recognized "his sock, Roberto's rib." She felt his presence with her. "When I saw the first piece of my son, I knew it was him. It had his essence, his scent, he was there, and I dug, I wanted to get everything I could find . . . but all of a sudden I had to leave, I had to stop digging. Ten yards away I found his hand. After three years, imagine! And another ten yards from there was part of his foot."

The remains of her son Roberto were sent to a laboratory, and after forty days, she received the genetic confirmation that her instinct had not lied: "I never said, 'Maybe it's him.' I always said it was him. And now my son is at rest, just as I promised him."

The group's motto was "We will search for you until we find you." She had done it, but she kept on working, pushing that rod into the ground in order to detect the smell of death. "We have found ninety-six treasures," she said. "Forty-one of those treasures belonged to the Trackers; the others belonged to people who were not in the group. Many women who have found their treasures keep working, like me. We support other women."

When she heard the news, Griselda Triana called Mirna and told her, "I know Javier is up in heaven holding his hat and dancing around, he's saying you did it, damn, woman, you did it!" Mirna said, "And it's true, I think he's up there and he's happy, because I did what I set out to do, I kept the promise I made to my son, I searched for him until I found him."

Meanwhile, *Ríodoce* was not giving up. "Aside from taking away our friend, they also took away the freedom to do our work, to go out and report every day like we used to. We lost that assurance completely," said Miriam Ramírez, surrounded by towering piles of paper at the weekly's office. In spite of everything, "what motivates us is the love we have for Javier; we are not willing to let his assassination go unpunished. That is the engine that drives us to keep going here, that's why no one has quit: it's for Javier, and the commitment we have to the public. We are so full of pain, full of anger, we are scared, but we will not be silent."

When I visited *Ríodoce*'s offices in Culiacán, Bojórquez offered me some tequila from a bottle Javier had left in his office. It was the very last sip: it had taken months to finish the bottle. It saddened him to drink from it. It seemed like not much had changed. A sign that Javier had made was still fixed to the outside wall of his cubicle. It read: "Investigation Unit/(Unit of one)."

A year later, on Christmas Day, 2018, his wife would post on Facebook: "There's sadness, pain, and anger, because you should be here, but there's one thing you can be sure of: I will not give up, I will not concede until we get justice, Javier."

10

The End of the Telenovela

"Before my speech, I would like us to observe a moment of silence for all of the people, the journalists, and the defenders of human rights who, sadly, while performing their work, their struggle, have fallen while carrying out their duty to which they had dedicated themselves," said President Enrique Peña Nieto. It was May 17, 2017, two days after the murder of Javier Valdez, and the president had called a meeting with ambassadors, governors, and cabinet secretaries to promise what had already been promised years ago: justice for the journalists and activists who had lost their lives.

"We will act resolutely to arrest and punish those responsible. A full democracy requires that no one silence their voice," he said, and then proceeded to coopt the slogan of many protests: "You can't kill the truth killing journalists." Some of the reporters who were present broke the ensuing silence with cries of "Justice!" although viewers watching the live transmission on television would never have known. The technicians broadcasting it had muted the sound.

But the president who was so devastated by Javier's assassination, who declared himself an ally of journalism, was a changed man just five weeks later. He was angry, even offended, by the journalists and the activists who had the nerve to accuse his government of wrongdoing.

According to an explosive investigation by the *New York Times*, Mexico's R3D, SocialTIC and Article 19, and Canada's Citizen Lab, the Mexican government spent $80 million on spyware known as Pegasus, made by the NSO Group. The Israeli cyberware company sold the software to governments "with an explicit agreement that it can be used only to battle terrorists or the drug cartels and criminal groups that have long kidnapped and killed Mexicans." The software had been used to track down El Chapo, but it had also been deployed for a very different purpose. It had been used against journalists, activists, human rights defenders. It had been used "against some of the government's most outspoken critics and their families."

In each case, the target would be sent a message designed to cause panic and compel the recipient to click on a link, through which the hackers would gain access to the target's cellphone. Carmen Aristegui was one such target. She was sent a message, purportedly from the U.S. Embassy in Mexico, instructing her to click on a link to resolve an issue with her visa. The wife of a well-known anti-corruption activist was also targeted with a message "claiming to offer proof that he was having an extramarital affair." A day after Javier Valdez was killed, his colleagues at *Ríodoce* received messages saying the killers had been arrested: it was a lie, but it served to take control of their cellphones.[1] Javier's wife, Griselda Triana, also received messages, including one that read: "The attorney general believes the motive of the Valdez murder was to steal his car." There was a link ostensibly to *Proceso* and *Animal Político*, and this allowed hackers access to her phone.[2]

According to the *New York Times*, through Pegasus it was possible "to monitor every detail of a person's cellular life—calls, texts, email, contacts and calendars." It could even "use the microphone and camera on phones for surveillance, turning a target's smartphone into a personal bug."[3]

The government initially denied the *New York Times* report, claiming that there was no evidence that it had illegally targeted citizens. A formal complaint was then lodged to the attorney general by Aristegui Noticias, the Mexican Institute for Competitiveness, the Pro Human Rights Center, Mexicans Against Corruption and Impunity, and El Poder del Consumidor, to request that the perpetrators be identified. Government espionage is a serious crime, punishable by prison sentences of six to twelve years.

The president responded as if he were the offended party: "It's very easy to get a group together to say the government is an entity that spies. Nothing could be further from the truth. I hope that the attorney general can, expeditiously, determine responsibilities, and I hope that, under the law, they can quickly apply it against those who have raised these false accusations against the government."[4]

The scandal was by no means the only one to rock the government. Individual reporters continued to do their best, connecting through WhatsApp groups, where they exchanged information and provided mutual support in the face of continued aggression from the state. They also circulated information on sources who otherwise would have had a very challenging time contacting the press directly.

One of the largest scandals came two and a half months after the revelations about Pegaus. Journalists uncovered what they dubbed "the Master Scam," involving 11 public agencies, 128 shell companies, 8 universities, a number of private companies, and 50 public servants, who embezzled at least $400 million from donors. The system had functioned for years and was detected as early as 2010 by government auditors, but both the Calderón and Peña Nieto administrations neglected to pursue judicial proceedings.

The website Animal Político and the group Mexicans Against Corruption and Impunity forced federal and state agencies to hand over reports of public spending and conducted hundreds of interviews in order to unravel the complex network, publishing the story in September 2017.[5] The impact of this report might have been more damaging to the president, but the government received some unexpected help: the court of public opinion was swiftly redirected when, on September 19, a devastating earthquake of an estimated magnitude of 7.1 struck central Mexico, killing an estimated 370 and injuring more than 6,000.

Even in the immediate aftermath of the earthquake, as bodies were being pulled from the rubble, there were blatant attempts by the administration to spin the news in their favor through their media allies, such as Televisa. The most embarrassing was possibly the case of Frida Sofía.

No one has been able to determine exactly where the rumor started that a five-year-old girl, named Frida Sofía, had been located, still alive, in the ruins of a collapsed school in southern Mexico City. There were apparently five other trapped children near her. At least, that was what was reported by Televisa reporter Danielle Dithurbide, who had exclusive access to the story. The Secretary of the Navy, in charge of rescue and relief efforts, did not explain why only she and her team were granted access, while all other journalists had to rely on second-hand information.

Frida Sofía captured the hope of all Mexicans. Throughout the day, Dithurbide interviewed volunteers who claimed they had talked to the girl or had heard her voice. She interviewed rescue workers who confirmed they had located the girl and her classmates with trained dogs and heat-sensing cameras. She also reported that the Navy had called the girl's parents, who were not at the site.

Two admirals corroborated the story. "We have identified a person, a minor, on the second floor of the collapsed building," explained Admiral José Luis Vergara, "She is alive, but the situation is highly unstable." Beside him, Admiral Ángel Enrique Sarmiento, Assistant Secretary of the Navy, confirmed that "they have been hydrating her since this morning with water through a hose."

The Rébsamen School was the place to be seen, and by the evening of that day, Peña Nieto and three of his cabinet members who were aspiring to his position arrived at the site and spoke exclusively with Televisa, clarifying that there were still four people alive, a teacher and three students who had managed to take shelter underneath a granite table in the kitchen.

The following morning, Carmen Aristegui aired several interviews questioning the blockbuster story. She spoke with Edgardo del Villar of Telemundo, who explained he had not been able to find "any original or official source that could confirm the [Frida] story," and a woman identified as Luz, who said her husband had gone in the area early that morning and "there never was a girl."

Then, suddenly, with no explanation, Televisa forgot all about

Frida and broadcast from other disaster zones. Admiral Sarmiento claimed he never said what he had said: "The version that came out with the name of a girl, we have no knowledge of that, we never had any knowledge of that version, and we are sure it was not real." Televisa rejected an onslaught of accusations of "staging a reality show," with a statement read in sober tones by the two news anchors in charge of the story. "We are completely stunned and offended," they said, and going off-script, they listed the aspects of the story had struck them as strange—that the parents of the girl had not appeared, that they had been given conflicting information about her location, that the number of trapped children changed over forty-eight hours. They did not explain how it was that they never asked Dithurbide to verify what had happened. They had stuck to the kind of journalism they usuall practiced, the kind that does not investigate, but simply repeats what authorities spouts.

The presidential elections were still 9 months away. Polls of voters were closely scrutinized, especially since several of the organizations that had conducted surveys in 2012 were accused of lying to give the impression that Peña Nieto's victory was a foregone conclusion. But this time Andrés Manuel López Obrador was without doubt the one to beat, and not only because he was in the lead. In his two previous presidential campaigns, the factions comprising the political-economic power elite had joined forces around one of his rivals to ensure his defeat, first supporting Felipe Calderón (PAN) in 2006, and then Peña Nieto (PRI) in 2012. Now, the two major parties opposing him were wracked by internal divisions. Former members of both parties were running as independent candidates, including Margarita Zavala (ex-PAN, wife of Calderón) and Jaime Rodríguez Calderón (ex-PRI), undermining support for the candidates of their former parties, Ricardo Anaya (of PAN and in coalition with two smaller partners) and José Antonio Meade (of PRI and in coalition with two smaller allies).

During the campaign, AMLO was a target of the same attacks that had damaged him in the past: commentators said he was dangerous for Mexico; he would turn the country into another Venezuela; he would cause an exodus of investment capital and a currency devaluation. There were new lines of attack: he was part of a new global wave of populist leaders and would be Mexico's version of Trump. But this time he proved to be immune. "They can say what they want," he said, "but they could never say I'm inconsistent, much less a crook."

A fundamental component of his platform was honesty—in sharp contrast to the obfuscating corruption of traditional Mexican politics—and he was able to uphold this image in spite of some uncharacteristic moves. He had always denounced what he called "the mafia of power," but this time he made concessions that would have seemed unthinkable in the past. He formed political alliances with people and organizations that would have in the past seemed hostile to him, such as the wealthy business magnate Alfonso Romo, who took charge of winning the support of other powerful multimillionaires, as well as political forces he had previously rejected as dishonest. For example, he received support from Elba Esther Gordillo, the controversial leader of the 1.6-million-strong teachers' union. Twelve years before, when contested official results gave Calderón a victory by the narrow margin of 0.5 percent, AMLO could have used Gordillo's support, turning the outcome to his benefit, but he wouldn't even meet her to talk.

Naturally, the media played a pivotal role in the lead up to the elections, raising the question of one of the main sources of corruption and wasteful spending among politicians, patrons, and the media—the sale of advertising on radio and television to political parties and candidates. In 2007, there were moves by politicians and civil society leaders to try and eliminate it, but media companies, advertising companies, and political candidates managed to circumvent this by means such as anonymous donations or the cash sale of "packages," including coverage and interviews to promote or disparage certain people, subjects, and platforms. This was easy to do because, according to an analysis of the front pages of six dailies with national circulation over 2016, about half of the content was based on interviews or hearsay rather than actual reporting. "The newspapers that dedicated the largest percentage of their front pages to what was said are, in several cases, also the main beneficiaries of spending on media: *El Sol de México* (71%), *Milenio* (68%), *Excélsior* (58%), *La Jornada* (46%), *El Universal* (40%) and *Reforma* (31%)." The report found that, "after patronage, payment for coverage is one of the areas campaigns spend on the most, always illegally, because it is an expense prohibited by law."[6]

The National Electoral Institute (INE) is responsible for detecting bias and imbalance, but the media had their ways of avoiding its scrutiny, especially when it came to television and radio. Moreover, the INE focused on the campaigning period, whereas, in practice, the use of government budgets to reward loyalty and punish detractors is hardly restricted to the campaigning period.

An analysis by the research center Fundar revealed that, between 2013 and 2016, the Peña Nieto administration disproportionately benefited certain favorite media conglomerates, with Grupo Televisa topping the list by receiving 19 percent of the total spending on government advertising, followed by Televisión Azteca (almost 11 percent), the newspaper *Excélsior* (3.6 percent), Starcom Worldwide (3 percent), and Radio Fórmula (2.5 percent). Just eight companies accounted for half of the federal government's advertising spending in this period.[7] *The New York Times* summed up the panorama in the blunt headline of a story in December 2017, which detailed how $2 billion had been spent: "Using Billions in Cash, Mexico Controls News Media."[8]

Peña Nieto had promised to regulate official advertising in his 2012 campaign and had agreed to include it as part of his political reforms in 2014. Legislation was put forth but it failed to pass into law. In November 2017, Article 19 Mexico succeeded in convincing the Supreme Court to impose a deadline on Congress—April 2018—to draft and pass the legislation. The collective #MediosLibres, comprised of eighty-five civil, academic, and business organizations, proposed defining criteria for awarding official advertising money with transparency and oversight.[9] They were ignored. The statute that legislators finally passed was a charade that "does not meet the criteria established in the terms" and "legalizes bad practices."[10]

The group's condemnation went unnoticed, like the killing of five journalists that took place during the five months of political campaigning in 2018. The Article 19-led network #RompeElMiedo (break fear), which established a monitoring system to protect reporters covering politics, documented 388 aggressions in those five months, of which almost half were linked to the elections. The main aggressors in these cases were public officials and members of political parties, or their sympathizers.[11] Freedom of expression, the public's right to be informed, and violence against the press were subjects as wholly absent from campaign debates as the regulation of government advertising. The presidential candidates did not talk about them even once.

On July 1, 2018, the election results confirmed the PRI's and PAN's worst nightmare: with 53 percent of the votes, AMLO was victor in every state except one, winning majorities in both chambers of the Congress of the Union and in many state congresses, and his MORENA-led coalition won five governorships. PAN and its allies trailed by around thirty points, with 22 percent. PRI, the party that had enjoyed seventy-one years of single-party rule and had been the ruling party for the past six, was trounced by over 35 points—it only got 16 percent, the worst result since its founding in 1929.

Peña Nieto's approval rating had been 57 percent in May 2013, about six months into his term, but the ongoing violence, the numerous corruption scandals, the spike in gas prices, the incomprehensible blunder of inviting then presidential candidate Donald Trump to visit Mexico in 2016—all investigated by independent journalists—among many other factors, drove his approval ratings into freefall until they bottomed out at 18 percent in August 2018, the worst ever registered for a Mexican president.[12]

Two days before the end of his term, on November 28, 2018, Peña Nieto subjected the country to one last humiliation. Journalists and intellectuals had mounted a rare alliance in condemning

Trump's visit two years earlier and they were unified once again when the outgoing president awarded Mexico's highest honor bestowed on foreigners, the Order of the Aztec Eagle, to Jared Kushner, Donald Trump's son-in-law. "It is a supreme act of humiliation and cowardice," conservative historian Enrique Krauze tweeted. "It's the perfect finale for his term," said academic Carlos Bravo Regidor, "a perfect illustration of his administration's degradation with respect to Trump."

The disapproval that informed the elections was not limited to the president; it applied to the entire political system. Corruption, authoritarianism, and arrogance had flourished under Pena Nieto. The independent press revealed countless crimes and cases of fraud, but so much remains hidden. But they did open millions of voters' eyes to the reality of this political and economic system, and they made the system pay. Yet journalists continue to die. The people who die to open society's eyes, their deaths continue to go unrecognized and unseen.

▌▌
The Beginning of a New Regime

"In the name of the Mexican state, we offer a public apology for the violation of your human rights, within the context of exercising the right to freedom of expression." It was January 11, 2019, and Deputy Secretary of Human Rights Alejandro Encinas was addressing journalist Lydia Cacho. This act of contrition was for five offenses: violating the right to freedom of expression; arbitrary detention; torture as a means of interrogation; gender-based violence and discrimination; and impunity and corruption fomented by government institutions.

Quite an inventory had accumulated over thirteen years. In her book *The Demons of Eden*, published in 2005, Lydia exposed a child sexual exploitation network that involved nineteen government officials and business leaders, headed by the Lebanese-born businessman Jean Succar Kuri with the help of Kamel Nacif—a Mexican of Lebanese descent. They were protected by politicians such as Miguel Ángel Yunes Linares, then deputy secretary of Federal Public Security and from 2016 to 2018 the governor of Veracruz. Nacif sued Cacho for defamation, not in Cancún, where she lived and where the child prostitution ring was based, but 740 miles away in Puebla (the capital of the state of Puebla), where he had Governor Mario Marín's support. In December 2005, a dozen Puebla state police officers and armed civilians abducted Cacho and transported her from Cancún, across five state lines, over a period of twenty hours, subjecting her to violence and verbal abuse. They brought her to a Puebla jail, where prison inmates were instructed to rape her with a broom handle. Luckily, two determined female prison guards saved her from this fate, locking Cacho in the infirmary for her own protection.

The newspaper *La Jornada* published audio recordings of telephone conversations between Marín and Nacif, who flatters Marín with phrases like "my precious governor" and "you're the hero in this movie," and between Nacif and others in which, in bluntly misogynist terms, they discuss in detail their plans to "give that old bitch a good whack," with the help of key allies, including judges, prosecutors, and media outlets.[1] Andrés Becerril of *Milenio Diario* was also caught speaking with Nacif on tape. "I'm going to drive her crazy, until that lady begs for mercy," Nacif said, and the reporter replied, "Alright. You know I'll do whatever you want." Becerril acted as Nacif's mouthpiece, writing what Nacif told him to write.[2] Although he was fired when his role in the case was revealed, he was immediately snapped up by the newspaper *Excélsior*, which has allowed him to continue working as a journalist for fourteen more years.

In November 2007, at six votes to four, the Supreme Court of Justice of the Nation acknowledged that wrongful acts and rights violations had been committed against Lydia Cacho, but decided they were not serious and did not require a ruling from the court. The "precious governor" had mobilized the highest ranks of the PRI party, who pressured the judges to deliver a favorable resolution.[3]

More than a decade passed before justice would be finally served. In July 2018, the United Nations Human Rights Committee passed a resolution demanding that Mexico repair the damage done to the journalist, prosecute those responsible for the crimes committed against her, and abolish the slander and defamation statutes in state penal codes. At the time, even though the PRI had been defeated just days before, Peña Nieto was still in power.

The ceremony "publicly admitting Mexican State responsibility and issuing a public apology" took place six weeks into AMLO's new term, with high-ranking officials from the United Nations, the Mexican ambassador to the United Nations, and the director of Article 19 (Cacho's legal representative) in attendance. The new secretary of the interior, Olga Sánchez Cordero, had been one of the six Supreme Court justices who voted against Cacho in 2007, and now presided over the event, announcing significant changes in the department that had traditionally dedicated itself to controlling the media: "This act represents the start of a state policy committed to reporters. Censorship will never again have a place in this Secretary of the Interior."

Cacho did not personally reproach anyone, instead emphasizing the significance of "the biggest fight I've ever fought in my life" in constructing the country's future: "This administration has the responsibility to use the next six years to establish the real rule of law. This will only be possible if leaders in every part of the country believe they must admit the truth and not create alternative, self-serving realities.

"My generation—I'm fifty-five—came into newspaper journalism when sexist jokes and harassment were common. We were told journalism was men's work; that human rights were feminine;

that children's voices did not belong in the newspaper. No one can take that accomplishment away from us. Though tortured and harassed, we do not have to submit to a corrupt, dishonest, sexist version of journalism, complacent with patriarchal power. Women have arrived to change this country's history."

From its earliest days, the López Obrador administration signaled that it wanted to change the executive office's relationship with the press. He vowed to end censorship and give full rein to freedom of expression; he announced he would cut government advertising spending to half of what had been spent under Peña Nieto; he aimed to support smaller media outlets with indigenous and local community perspectives; and he named new directors of public media, including some with a demonstrated commitment to democratizing the press, insisting they will have editorial independence and serve the public, not the government.

This comes as media companies face a general crisis, as traditional network television declines in the face of competition from streaming platforms, as well as corporate restructuring, and the prospect that government advertising money, which in the past had flowed generously to reward political loyalty, would now be redirected elsewhere. If the latter were to become a reality, Grupo Televisa, for example, would lose one of the main supports that helped it stay afloat.

The new president's style of communication is radically different from that of his predecessors. Every morning at seven, he holds an event colloquially known as *la mañanera* (the morning session), which is broadcast live on television and online. During his first ten weeks in office, AMLO probably held more press conferences than Peña Nieto, Calderón, and Fox combined. By February 18, 2019, he had held fifty-six mañaneras within seventy-nine days, according to reporter Ernesto Núñez: he had been asked 1,075 questions, and the president had spent seventy-one hours and fifty-three minutes answering them.

On the one hand, this seems like an unprecedented effort to establish transparency in a country where presidents never held public discussions with legislators and rarely allowed questions from journalists. On the other hand, there have been complaints about what some see as a disruptive presence. In Núñez's words, AMLO sets "the public agenda, chooses the subjects of conversation on social media, and constructs a daily narrative." Also, "he disrupts the working dynamic of the media, making the morning papers seem outdated by seven in the morning," with the same effect on radio news scripts and morning news shows on television.

Adapting to the new practices has been challenging. Reporters are not used to questioning the president in front of a massive live audience. And the public has never before been able to closely observe the day-to-day work of journalism. Opinion on the quality of the questioning runs quick and harsh. The president's sympathizers interpret the simplest questions as attacks on him: on social media mobs of trolls accuse even reporters with the longest track records defending human rights of being far-right militants.

For their part, some political, intellectual, and civic activists feel like they are constantly under attack: while saying he respects opinions that aren't his own, AMLO asserts his right to participate in public discussion and respond to questions directly. This may be commonplace in places that enjoy head-to-head debate, such as in the United Kingdom, but it is disconcerting to the

Mexican sensibility, with its delicate formality. In Mexico, we are used to having a president residing somewhere above the clouds, far above us mere mortals. López Obrador has clearly broken from this tradition. People are annoyed by his labeling of those who criticize or reject his plans and decisions, from politicians or intellectuals to media outlets and civil organizations, as "conservative," or his use of terms such as *fifís* (referring to superficial, rich people) to criticize his detractors. There is no lack of people who see in this behavior evidence that, just as they had warned, AMLO will eventually reveal himself to be another Hugo Chávez. To his supporters, however, that reaction is nothing more than the foot-stamping tantrums of the privileged members of the regime's inner circle, who were once on the receiving end of handouts and now feel pushed aside.

The value of criticism in the democratic process is little understood in this country, on the right and the left. Habituated to the patrimonial use of power, the political right in its various forms has never tolerated journalistic criticism beyond what it considered appropriate. This could be seen in Peña Nieto's actions as president when he censored Carmen Aristegui and took an aggressive stance against those who accused his government of spying. On the left, generally, there is no clear concept of what role the media should play in a democracy, especially now. For a century leftists and dissidents have been punished by what they justifiably call *prensa vendida*, a "bought-and-paid-for press," which has dominated the public sphere. The "critical press" is expected to reflexively support social movements, to cover issues affecting vulnerable populations and political resistance, under the assumption that they are unquestionably fair and incorruptible. It is seen as something instrumental to social and political movements on the left, especially now the left now is in power.

The inevitable disappointment that comes from this provokes immediate, aggressive, and little considered reactions, and the entire career of a journalist or media outlet can be trashed, especially through social media, the minute any dissonance is detected, no matter how minor. In the first months of the new administration, the impact of this was magnified by the creation of phenomena such as #RedAMLOve, in which bots and trolls coordinated attacks on critics of the government.[4]

Any unconditional support on the part of the press would be a betrayal of their responsibility not only to the public but also to the social movements themselves, which in no case—at any point in history, in any place in the world—are ever beyond the possibility of misappropriation and corruption. These movements' purest goals are best protected by an active press ready to uncover errors and abuses. To me, *Proceso* remains an emblematic example of what this entails: if many AMLO voters hoped the magazine would become a mouthpiece for the new administration (Julio Scherer Ibarra, the eldest son of the publication's late founder, is the president's legal advisor), the weekly has taken pains to distance itself and remain critical of the presidency, even as the pressure on the media has only intensified with AMLO's popularity. He won 53 percent of the vote in the July election, and from there the president's popularity has soared to unprecedented levels, with a consensus among polls of around an 80 percent approval rating after his first hundred days in office.

Like other leaders, AMLO exploits tension as a means to keep his supporters mobilized. His immense popularity gives him cover. He seems to have made a decision to keep opposition parties out of the spotlight. He ignores them while using dissidents from academia and the media as sparring partners. In the United States, this echoes Donald Trump and his daily rants against the "failed" *New York Times*, CNN, *Washington Post*, and others. But the similarities end there. In his morning press conferences, AMLO sometimes evades, pushes back, and distracts, but there is a wide distance between him and a habitual lying bully like Trump. The occupant of the White House tells people to act against his "treasonous" critics; the man in the Palacio Nacional insists "journalists are free" and vows to protect freedom of expression. Between D.C. and Mar-a-Lago, one maintains a cosmic distance from the people he governs; between his apartment in the middle-class neighborhood Copilco, Mexico City, and the places across the country he travels every week, the other flies economy on commercial flights, and talks to his fellow travelers, even taking selfies with people who approach him.

In any case, there is no denying that AMLO is stubborn, and we should not expect him to change. We will have to get used to the new presidential style of arguing against opinions and with information that he finds either inconvenient or contradictory to his own, whether his arguments are well-founded or not. If what feels like undue pressure on us makes us uncomfortable, we have the option to produce better journalism than play his game.

And it is possible we are giving this issue more attention than it deserves, since the most urgent matters for journalists are violence, labor instability, corruption, and censorship: the real persecutors of freedom of expression. In the worst time period in journalism history in Mexico, the six months between March and August

2017, ten journalists were killed, attempts were made on the lives of three others (one bodyguard did not survive), one was wounded by a gunshot, a foreign television crew was kidnapped and robbed, an organized mob attacked, kidnapped, and robbed seven reporters in Guerrero, we complained because the government spied on our phones, then an indignant Peña Nieto ordered the spies to take action against the spied on. That can never be repeated. Still, what should set off alarms is that, in the first five months after AMLO took office, five reporters were killed, and by the end of 2019, ten journalists had been killed, one more than in 2018 and just two less than 2017, the worst year.

Journalism and freedom of expression are under attack across the globe. Aspiring despots of every stripe abound, from the United States' Donald Trump, Brazil's Jair Bolsonaro, Nicaragua's José Daniel Ortega Saavedra, and Venezuela's Nicolás Maduro to Turkey's Recep Tayyip Erdogan, Saudi Arabia's Mohammed bin Salman, Egypt's Abdel Fattah al-Sisi, Russia's Vladimir Putin, and China's Xi Jinping. Out in the streets, police no longer distinguish between those setting cars on fire and those taking photos; intelligence services have the press in their crosshairs; jails around the world are filling up with reporters. Journalists are assassinated and the killers get away with it. The Mexican government under Peña Nieto was hardly the only one among self-congratulating "democracies" where authorities violate fundamental democratic principles by intimidating journalists. As impunity grows, it is left to the public, and not the media, to protest and demand justice.

In order for the mainstream press to carry out its duty to serve society and safeguard it against the abuses of power, it must

216 KILLING THE STORY

recover society's support, which has been lost in good measure because it has rarely prioritized serving the public. Instead, it has prioritized the very power that bribes it, harasses it, and ultimately suppresses it.

The Italian Marxist philosopher Antonio Gramcsi in his *Prison Notebooks* wrote of the role of the organic intellectual—every class produces its own intellectuals in an "organic" way, and they serve as its spokespeople articulating views that the class may not be able to express for themselves. As Mexican journalist Ricardo Raphael has argued, if the ruling class produces its organic intellectuals who profit from their proximity to power, these intellectuals are not there to produce independent, critical knowledge, "out of science," as Gramsci would say. If the press takes this role, society cannot expect it to serve society as a whole but the class they came from, the one in power. Raphael wrote:

> Power's lackeys are organically corrupt intellectuals. They commit criminal conspiracy against the public treasury because they live off of it and bite their tongues, because they fight desperately to be advisors to the prince, because they do not have the courage to tell the truth and, above all, because they add no social value. Spokespersons for the political class are propagandists, condescending loudmouths uninterested in the accuracy, responsibility and consequences of their actions.[5]

This was clear under the PRI and PAN. Will something similar take place under AMLO? There is real danger when eras change their dress. Again, in Gramsci's terms, between one segment of history and another, one may fear the most cynical will reveal the worst opportunism: "The old world dies. The new one is late in coming. And in this fog the monsters rise."[6] If the powerful popular movement that allowed AMLO to overcome the obstacles in his path is to succeed in deeply changing Mexico for better, it will only do it with a critical press that investigates and reports on the ineptitudes, negligence, abuse, and excesses of those in power, and that includes AMLO's administration. No one can claim to be immune.

The first steps are for the federal government to stop using its official advertising budget as part of a carrot-and-stick strategy, as it has announced it would, and for a similar plan to be enacted on the state and municipal level. Media outlets will have to learn how to survive from other revenue streams, from private advertisers, their readers and audiences, and other sources. They will have to acknowledge that for decades they have reaped tremendous rewards by exploiting their personnel, and they must improve their relationship with their employees. Then they will win their independence.

Meanwhile, some prominent figures from the bought-and-paid-for press have fallen. New spaces have opened up, and they must be taken. Mexico can support a more diverse journalism, instead of pushing critical voices out to the margins as the elites have done. For example, the daily *Reforma* named an activist who was spied on by Pegasus as its editorial director, to establish itself as the voice of the business world that does not trust AMLO. That is a valid choice, based on freedom of expression, even though it does not please everyone.

Looking ahead, AMLO's rhetoric again censorship and in favor of freedom of the press would be better appreciated if the situation changed on the ground for journalists. How long do we have to wait until they can put a stop to the crimes committed against journalists? And how long do we have to wait until they bring those people who have committed these crimes with impunity to justice?

In July 21, 2019, six months after the Mexican State publicly apologized to her, Lydia Cacho received a death threat and unidentified individuals broke into her home and stole a laptop computer, audio recorder, three cameras, several memory cards, and ten hard drives containing information about sexual abuse cases. Mario Marín, the former State of Puebla governor who illegally jailed her and ordered her to be raped, was seen at a PRI public meeting, despite police seeking his arrest. After this incident, Lydia went abroad. She remains in exile at the time of writing. Her aggressors are roaming free.

EPILOGUE

Bernardo Torres works as a photographer and videographer in one of the most dangerous states for journalism, Guerrero. There you have to watch out for criminal gangs, the police, vigilante groups, companies with paramilitary protection, and business leaders, politicians, and public officials, like Javier Duarte, who see freedom of expression as only an impediment, buying people off and crushing whoever refuses to be bought.

On November 24, 2016, a dozen reporters were caught in the crossfire between two vigilante militias, the Union of Peoples and Organizations of Guerrero State (UPOEG) and the United Front for the Security and Development of Guerrero (FUSDEG). Both organizations have racked up numerous crimes and have even committed massacres (I personally covered one carried out by FUSDEG, in which nine people from the village of Xolapa were killed on June 6, 2015). A week later, Bernardo Torres took me to the spot on the highway, near Tierra Colorada, where they had taken cover behind a pickup truck. From there they had alerted authorities and transmitted the shootout live, bullets flying right past them, as they screamed, "Press! We're the press!" From the first shot that rang out at six in the morning until the last at four in the afternoon, no one from the federal or state police, or the Army or the Navy intervened, even though they all worked on a joint security operation in the state. The gun fight continued, killing at least one man and injuring several others. "About 500 meters away, there were some patrol cars out front there, but no, they didn't get involved," Joaquina Nava, the owner of a small family restaurant nearby, told me. "We thought they had killed a journalist because we heard them yelling and we thought they had killed him, but we couldn't find out because we were lying down on the ground. We didn't find out because we were afraid. The police never came."

"Yes, the FUSDEG commander, who came to support his men, he told us about it the next day," Torres said. "He had an automatic weapon. He told us: 'when I saw the pickup, I was going to grab it and fire on them, the ones who were there; I was ready. But I got closer and saw the logos on the truck and I stopped. Then I saw there were cameras, they were holding up cameras, that was when I told my men to hold their fire so they could leave. But if it hadn't been for that, I would have shot them, I would have killed them.'"

Just as in Veracruz, Oaxaca, and other regions, journalists in Guerrero try to move around in groups for security, and also to save money. Their salaries are extremely low, and any costs incurred related to their work come out of their own pockets. The best-paid staff reporters earn as much as 8,000 pesos a month (450 dollars), but the ones at news agencies don't earn any more than 3,000 pesos (180 dollars), and they must write four articles per day, explained Bernardo Torres: "With the social media boom, now they don't just ask for a story, they want photos and video too. For the same pay. And they don't provide any equipment. Camera, phone, cars, gas: all of that comes out of your pocket." Precariousness, as Ruben

Espinosa always said, remains one of the greatest challenges journalism faces.

So given the financial hardships, the risks to both your own safety and that of your friends and family, the physically and psychologically taxing working conditions that lead to frustration and burnout in a job that can seem to have no effect whatsoever in the short term, having saved no lives nor protected any community from harm, why be a journalist in this day and age? Or if you are a journalist, why not sell out?

When I was a student, I admired three journalists who now personify the bought-and-paid-for press: Carlos Marín, who had reported on the government's death squads; Ricardo Alemán, who laid bare the mechanisms of corruption in journalism and wrote some of the most revealing and amusing stories on Congress; and Ciro Gómez Leyva, who helped to unmask the pedophilia of the founder of the Legion of Christ, Marcial Maciel, and along with his colleagues faced devastating reprisals set in motion by Lorenzo Servitje, one of the wealthiest business magnates in Mexico. What would those three say now to their twenty-one-year-old selves, so full of talent back then, so determined, so brave? Could they look them in the eye? Or would they avoid them, fearing the young men would excoriate them because their older selves represented everything a journalism student should fight against?

I remember back in 1999, Salvador Frausto, Alejandro Olmos, another colleague, and I got together with Ricardo Alemán in a dive bar called La Vitrola in Insurgentes Sur avenue, Mexico City. At the end of the night, in the late hour when alcohol lets loose unfiltered honesty—or cynicism—Alemán said to us, "Very soon, you're not even going to want to admit you know me." We didn't realize what he meant. The embittered adult betrayed himself and morphed into someone who, as Pablo Neruda put it, "is reflected in the world's mirror and his face is not pleasing even to himself."

What happened to them? Some would explain it away with a cliché: that the twenty-year-old who isn't an idealist has no heart, but the forty-year-old who's still an idealist has no brain. That is the argument of those who need to somehow justify not loving their own dreams enough.

A friend of mine told me that, aside from the money, these people were seduced by power. But if a politician, police chief, or military officer decides what information to give you, whether it's true or false, and determines when and how you publish it, that says that you, as the journalist, do not have power. They have the power. All you're doing is cutting and pasting. You're a gossip with a nice car. As journalist Yoloxóchitl Casas said to me, it's the transformation of sacred cows into beef cattle.

The disproportionate scale of the corruption from the recent past seems to dwarf investigative journalism's achievements. Those industrial media outlets that have the financial and human resources to launch large-scale projects are still more interested in ingratiating themselves to political and economic power than in revealing their misdeeds. That immense task falls to journalist collectives, foundations, independent outlets, and freelance reporters.

If accolades and winning awards are not a top priority for journalists, who should above all serve the society they report in, they are useful as a measure of the outsized impact the small sector of independent journalism has had, winning the top categories of the National Journalism Prizes in the six years of Peña Nieto's term, from 2013 to 2018. Looking back to appreciate these achievements is not banal, nor is it banal to consider that based on this collective work (journalism is, after all, a group passion), millions of citizens were able to make informed decisions and cast their vote in 2018. After years traveling around Mexico, looking for interview subjects, the members of Ojos de Perro can attest to the difficult working conditions, the financial hardships, and the security risks endured by journalists and their loved ones. But we wanted to find out why they continue to do journalism, what inspires them, what sustains them. You can see it, of course, in their work, but we were fortunate to be given some further glimpses from the journalists themselves or their loved ones.

> My brother said it's to show people the truth, the reality, not to hide it, so they know where we are, what's happening, what is actually going on.
>
> —*Patricia Espinosa, Rubén Espinosa's sister,*
> *Mexico City*

> A journalist is important because they are your eyes in another place and in a different way, it's the opportunity to see the situation, to look around you through different eyes, in a way that the government, probably, doesn't want you to.
>
> —*Jorge Sánchez, son of Moisés Sánchez,*
> *Medellín, Veracruz*

Michael Ignatieff says that when democracy fails, when the balance of power fails, when Congress is not able to tie his hands, to restrain the President, when Judicial Power is involved in the conflicts, there are two other institutions in a democracy that should play an active role and fill the void: communications media and the citizenry. If they are united I think it's much better. Those of us in the media have to ask ourselves: are we more on the public's side, or on the side of political power?

—Adrián López, director of the daily Noroeste, *in Culiacán, Sinaloa*

By definition, investigative journalism is always going to make power uncomfortable, no matter its party ideology.

—Daniel Lizárraga, former chief of Carmen Aristegui's Investigation Unit, Mexico City

If the people keep going, if the people get up to go to work, we journalists cannot stop doing our work. The people of Juárez are not telling us what we have to do. They go out, scared, with caution, but they do go out and go on with their lives.

—Rocío Gallegos, Journalists Network of Juárez, Juárez City, Chihuahua

Only we who love this profession and were born to do it survive.

—*Isaín Mandujano, Chiapas Paralelo, Tuxtla Gutiérrez, Chiapas*

It's very satisfying when you bring a problem to light, it gets resolved in your favor and the people are totally grateful, I think this is one of the best prizes you can get because you feel a part of them. To us, as Oaxacans, the land, the culture, the act of giving has always tremendously motivated us, and the people that give back is the least of it. That is what gratifies you, you say "it was worth it." This profession is one of the best decisions of my life.

—*Pedro Matías, Proceso correspondent, Oaxaca, Oaxaca*

I am happy. I like accomplishing something. That is what feeds your soul, you have that feeling that you did something good for someone else. Even though, we could say there are a host of problems behind you that you can't solve as a reporter, your problems as a reporter. But you could solve the public's problems.

—*Anonymous journalist in the central-south of Tamaulipas State*

These should serve as motivation for those who are now journalists, those who are studying journalism, and those wondering if they should enter the profession.

García Márquez saw himself as a reporter more than a novelist: "I believe my first and only vocation is journalism. I did not start off as a journalist by accident—as many people do—or out of necessity, or luck—I started as a journalist because what I wanted was to be a journalist." Those of us who were lucky enough to work with him enjoyed his approachable mentor-friend vibe, no matter that he was a Nobel Prize laureate, and learned from his living example as the most beautiful old man in the world that you can be true to yourself to the end.

"This is a very demanding profession," the Polish journalist Ryszard Kapuściński once warned. "They all are, but ours is in particular. That is because we live with it twenty-four hours a day. We can't close up our office at four in the afternoon and busy ourselves with other activities. This is a job that takes up our whole life, there is no other way to do it."

Not everyone has what it takes to be a journalist. It's a profession for deeply passionate people. But for those who feel it in their bones, who are ever-curious, resilient, resolute, they will discover it is their very nature that pushes them to journalism.

The journalist's power is to rise up before political and economic power; to get the information that power wants to hide and publish it so that the public can see—to serve the public interest. Remembering the young idealists we once were—the children we have protected from succumbing to despair—is useful when we take stock of ourselves, see the path we are on, and recalibrate the balance between our dreams and our deeds. The journalist demands justice, not vengeance. My colleagues and I will not capitulate under the harassment of any political party, as we watch the dawn of the new regime, hoping to tell the story of positive change, to be sure, and also with the full intention to continue working to reveal what power—which time and again over the course of history has been true to its corrosive nature—tries to keep hidden from the public.

We can embrace the children we once were. We can explain to them all we have done because we have not betrayed our dreams. We can reassure them that we will not give in or stop fighting. We sense that they will forgive us for our failures and still have hope for us. We look to the example of those who have fallen and those who resist, and preserve their passion for journalism, we look to the people in this book with the privilege to contribute to the world that journalism offers.

The children of today should motivate us, providing a sense of urgency to those of us who have not given up on working to fight for society's right to be informed. We do it for the ones who fought to win us the freedom of expression, for those who live on in their reporting, their stories, their spirit running like a current through our fingers as we type and take aim with our cameras, pushing us on.

"Even though you suffer like a dog, there is no better job than journalism," Gabriel García Márquez said. They will not shut us up. Journalism lives on.

ACKNOWLEDGMENTS

To those who opened the way for all of us and to those who have fallen in the struggle for freedom of speech and the right of society to be informed. To Jim, Moisés, Rubén, Nadia, Miroslava, Javier, Gary Webb, Daphne Caruana Galizia, the Charlie Hebdo's 12, and so many more.

To our colleagues who live under threat; to relatives, friends and reporting mates of the victims, who had the courage to give us their testimonies; to Colectivo Voz Alterna, Red de Periodistas de Juárez, Red Libre Periodismo de Chihuahua, Red de Periodistas del Noreste, Red de Periodistas Veracruzanos, Red de Periodistas Guerrerenses, and Chiapas Paralelo.

Of course, to my barking gang, Ojos de Perro vs la Impunidad (in particular the team I traveled with around Mexico: Juanfe Castro Gessner, Coizta Grecko, Yuli Rodríguez, Juanjo Rodríguez, Thalía Güido, Luis Alberto Castillo, and Humberto Ibarra), and to Cuadernos Doble Raya and Frontline Freelance Register.

To our sisters and brothers at Article 19 México, Red de Periodistas de a Pie, Committee to Protect Journalists, Reporters Without Borders, PEN Club, Fotorreporteros MX, and Derecho a Informar.

To my editors and translators, accomplices for the road: the late Gabriel García Márquez (I was international editor at his *Cambio* magazine in 2003 and 2004), Diane Stockwell, Ben Woodward and the team at The New Press, the late Óscar Hinojosa, the late Ramón Córdoba, Carlos Pedroza, Homero Campa, Salvador Frausto, Mael Vallejo, Iván Carrillo, Alberto Bello, Fernanda González, Enrique Murillo, Alejandro Pérez, Marta López, Manuel Martínez Torres, Hugo Martínez Téllez, Javier Martínez Staines, and Míriam Mabel Martínez (it seems I'd be unpublished without a Martínez near me!).

To Martín Caparrós, with whom I worked on the Moisés Sánchez chapter, and to the Fundación Gabriel García Márquez para el Nuevo Periodismo Iberoamericano that supported it.

To Armando Vega-Gil, friend, brother, and provocateur of happiness, in memoriam.

And, as always, to Beatriz and Roberto, chief culprits of my misdeeds.

NOTES

This book is mainly based on interviews conducted by the author with the following persons:

Adela Navarro (Tijuana, Baja California, November 24, 2016)

Adrián López (Mexico City, October 26, 2016)

Agustín Chávez (Carrillo Puerto, Quintana Roo, December 13, 2016)

Alicia Blanco (Tierra Blanca, Veracruz, January 3, 2017)

Anonymous photographer (Mexico City, July 26, 2016)

Arantxa Arcos (Mexico City, January 29, 2016)

Bernardo Torres (Tierra Colorada, Guerrero, December 3, 2016)

Carmen Aristegui (Mexico City, April 13, 2017)

Daniel Lizárraga (Mexico City, January 19, 2017)

Edison Lanza (Washington, D.C., May 27, 2016)

Elsa Pastor (Huajuapan de León, Oaxaca, January 5, 2017)

Enrique Juárez (undisclosed location, November 2016)

Ericka Olmos (Huajuapan de León, Oaxaca, January 5, 2017)

Erick Muñiz (Monterrey, Nuevo León, November 19, 2016)

Ernesto Ledesma (Mexico City, March 12, 2017)

Gabriela Minjares (Ciudad Juárez, Chihuahua, November 23, 2016)

Griselda Triana (Culiacán, Sinaloa, September 5, 2017)

Isaí Lara (Tijuana, Baja California, November 24, 2016)

Isaín Mandujano (Chiapa de Corzo, Chiapas, November 11, 2016)

Ismael Bojórquez (Culiacán, Sinaloa, September 7, 2017)

Israel Hernández (Veracruz, Veracruz, January 2, 2016)

Itzamná Ponce (Mexico City, July 26, 2016)

Javier Garza (Mexico City, October 26, 2016)

Jorge Sánchez (Medellín, Veracruz, April 28–29, 2015; Medellín and Xalapa, Veracruz, January 2–3, 2016; Medellín, Veracruz, January 2, 2017)

Juan David Castilla (Mexico City, January 29, 2016)

Juan Villoro (Mexico City, March 26, 2017)

Justin Dupuy (Mexico City, February 26, 2017)

Leopoldo Maldonado (Mexico City, January 18, 2017)

Lucy Sosa (Ciudad Juárez, Chihuahua, November 22, 2016)

Luis Alberto Cedillo (Monterrey, Nuevo León, November 19, 2016)

Melva Frutos (Monterrey, Nuevo León, November 19, 2016)

Miguel Turriza (Reynosa, Tamaulipas, November 20, 2016)

Míriam Ramírez (Culiacán, Sinaloa, September 7, 2017)

Myrna Nereyda Medina (Los Mochis, Sinaloa, September 6, 2017)

Noé Zavaleta (Xalapa, Veracruz, January 3, 2016)

Norma Madero (Cancún, Quintana Roo, December 14, 2016)

Norma Trujillo (Xalapa, Veracruz, January 3, 2016)

Patricia Espinosa (Mexico City, July 26, 2016)

Patricia Mayorga (Mexico City, October 12, 2018)

Pedro Canché (Carrillo Puerto, Quintana Roo, December 13, 2016)

Pedro Matías (Oaxaca, Oaxaca, January 4, 2016)

Rafael Rodríguez Castañeda (Mexico City, November 20, 2016)

Raziel Roldán (Mexico City, January 29, 2016)

Ricardo González (Mexico City, January 18, 2017)

Rigoberto Martínez(Huajuapan de León, Oaxaca, January 5, 2017)

Rocío Gallegos (Ciudad Juárez, Chihuahua, November 22, 2016)

Roger Martínez (Mexico City, January 29, 2016)

Also on interviews the Ojos de Perro's team members and collaborators had with:

Anonymous South-Central Tamaulipas journalist (undisclosed location, February 2017, by Juan Castro Gessner)

Jaime Armendáriz (Chihuahua, Chihuahua, September 4, 2017, by Coizta Grecko)

Noé Zavaleta (Ciudad de México, August 2, 2015, by Laurence Cuvillier)

Rolando Nájera (Chihuahua, Chihuahua, September 2, 2017, by Coizta Grecko)

Rubén Espinosa (Xalapa, Veracruz, April 28, 2015, by Laurence Cuvillier)

Introduction

1. Hugo Bachega, "Can Mexico Save Its Journalists?" BBC News, July 4, 2017, www.bbc.com/news/world-latin-america-39436568.

2. Bachega, "Can Mexico Save Its Journalists?"

1: Rubén Espinosa I

1. Sandra Rodríguez Nieto, "El perfil psicológico de Javier Duarte, un ladrón sin culpas," Sin Embargo, June 12, 2017, www.economiahoy.mx/nacional-eAm-mx /noticias/8424525/06/17/El-perfil-psicologico-de-Javier-Duarte-un-ladron-sin -culpas.html.

2. "Javier Duarte idolatra a Francisco Franco," May 10, 2010, YouTube video, www.youtube.com/watch?v=ZNoTp7v0tic.

3. Daniel Blancas, "Los Zetas mantienen presencia activa en 32 municipios de Veracruz," La Crónica, October 5, 2011, www.cronica.com.mx/notas/2012 /609613.html.

4. The protest at the Barcelona city hall was called by Deputy Mayor Gerardo Pisarello. Alejandro Gutiérrez, "Fidel Herrera dejó Barcelona como llegó: en el escándalo," Proceso, February 9, 2017, www.proceso.com.mx/473378/fidel-herrera -dejo-barcelona-llego-en-escandalo.

5. Article 19, "Periodistas asesinados en México," articulo19.org/periodistas asesinados; Article 19 MX-CA (@article19mex), "Periodistas desaparecidos en México," Twitter, September 16, 2017, twitter.com/article19mex/status /908829785610182656.

6. "Tres años de impunidad," Proceso, April 25, 2015, www.proceso.com.mx /402339/tres-anos-de-impunidad.

7. Periodistas de a Pie, "Amenazas contra periodistas en Veracruz y la libertad de expression," aired July 9, 2015, on Rompeviento TV, www.periodistasdeapie.org.mx /programa-92.php#; video available at www.mediafire.com/file/euvndxh4l5vh4re /Periodistas_de_a_Pie_-_09_de_julio_2015.mp4/file.

8. Pedro Canché, "'No quiero ser el número 13': Rubén Espinosa," Animal Político, August 3, 2015, www.animalpolitico.com/blogueros-blog-invitado/2015 /08/03/no-quiero-ser-el-numero-13-ruben-espinosa.

9. Daniela Rea, Mónica González, and Pablo Ferri, Investigation "Cadena de Mando," June 2016, cadenademando.org.

10. Ignacio Carvajal, "Todopoderosa, Gina premiaba a la prensa afín o casti-gaba; quitaba reporteros y manoseaba medios," Sin Embargo, May 21, 2017, www .sinembargo.mx/21-05-2017/3221486.

11. Noé Zavaleta, "Desaparición de 5 jóvenes es sólo 'una cosa que sale mal': Duarte," Proceso, January 19, 2016, www.proceso.com.mx/426989/para-duarte -desaparicion-de-5-jovenes-es-solo-una-cosa-que-sale-mal.

12. "Veracruz: Hundieron una varilla y dieron con la fosa más grande de México; ya llevan 287 cuerpos," Sin Embargo, April 2, 2018, www.sinembargo.mx/02-04 -2018/3403221.

13. "Premian a Duarte por proteger a periodistas," Animal Político, April 3, 2013, www.animalpolitico.com/2013/04/premian-a-duarte-por-proteger-a-periodistas -en-su-gobierno-han-asesinado-a-9.

14. Francisco Morales V., "Niega Rushdie respaldar a Javier Duarte," *Reforma*, October 7, 2014, www.reforma.com/aplicaciones/articulo/default.aspx?id =360247.

15. The sixteen are Alejandro Almazán, Elia Baltazar, Lolita Bosch, Daniela Rea Gómez, Diego Fonseca, Javier Garza, Ricardo González, Témoris Grecko, Diego Enrique Osorno, Emiliano Ruiz Parra, Daniela Pastrana, Rafael Pineda "Rapé," Wilbert Torre, Eileen Truax, Marcela Turati, and José Luis Valencia.

16. "Repudiamos el uso político del Hay Festival Xalapa," petition on change.org, February 2, 2015, www.change.org/p/repudiamos-el-uso-politico-del-hay-festival -xalapa.

17. "Repudiamos el uso político del Hay Festival Xalapa."

18. "Hay Festival dice adiós a Xalapa; su edición mexicana será digital," Aristegui Noticias, February 5, 2015, aristeguinoticias.com/0602/lomasdestacado/hay -festival-dice-adios-a-xalapa-su-edicion-mexicana-sera-digital.

19. "Amenazas contra el reportero Jorge Carrasco," *Proceso*, April 16, 2013, www .proceso.com.mx/339194/amenazas-contra-el-reportero-jorge-carrasco.

20. Excerpts from the interview with Nadia Vera, "Veracruz: la fosa olvidada," Rompeviento TV, November 26, 2014, youtu.be/XSTWoTz6oXU.

2: Rubén Espinosa II

1. Rubén Espinosa, "'La muerte escogió a Veracruz como su casa y decidió vivir ahí,' dice fotógrafo en el exilio," interview by Shaila Rosagel, Sin Embargo, July 1, 2015, www.sinembargo.mx/01-07-2015/1398019.

2. *Periodistas de a Pie*, "Amenazas contra periodistas en Veracruz y la libertad de expression," aired July 9, 2015, on Rompeviento TV, www.periodistasdeapie.org .mx/programa-92.php#.

3. Noé Zavaleta, *El infierno de Javier Duarte: Crónicas de un gobierno fatídico* (Mexico City: Ediciones Proceso, 2016), 135.

4. Espinosa, "'La muerte escogió a Veracruz como su casa y decidió vivir ahí.'"

5. Rubén Espinosa, "La última entrevista al fotógrafo mexicano Rubén Espinosa," interview by Noemí Redondo, Sin Filtros, July 25, 2016, www.sinfiltros.com /especiales/libertad-de-expresion/la-ultima-entrevista-del-fotografo-mexicano -ruben-espinosa-20160725.html.

6. Pablo De Llano, "Killing of Rubén Espinosa Leaves Mexican Journalists in

Fear," *El País*, August 4, 2015, english.elpais.com/elpais/2015/08/04/inenglish /1438688232_170340.html.

7. Pedro Canché, "'No quiero ser el número 13': Rubén Espinosa," Animal Político, August 3, 2015, www.animalpolitico.com/blogueros-blog-invitado/2015 /08/03/no-quiero-ser-el-numero-13-ruben-espinosa.

8. PEN America, "Presidente Nieto: Investigue los asesinatos de periodistas en México y establezca mecanismos para protegerlas," pen.org/presidente-nieto -investigue-los-asesinatos-de-periodistas-en-mexico-y-establezca-mecanismos-para -protegerlas.

9. "México: ¡Paremos los ataques a la libertad de expresión!," online petition at Avaaz, secure.avaaz.org/es/ruben_global_l/?slideshow.

10. Ricardo Alemán, "Fue un vulgar robo; nada implica a Duarte," *El Universal*, August 10, 2015, eluniversal.com.mx/entrada-de-opinion/columna/ricardo -aleman/nacion/2015/08/10/fue-un-vulgar-robo-nada-implica-duarte.

11. Ricardo Alemán, "Narvarte: Se refuerza línea de crimen por narcomenudeo," *El Universal*, August 16, 2015, www.eluniversal.com.mx/entrada-de-opinion /columna/ricardo-aleman/metropoli/df/2015/08/16/narvarte-se-refuerza-linea-de.

12. Ciro Gómez Leyva, "El departamento de Narvarte era también una casa de citas: Cinco personas muertas, el daño colateral de una desafortuanda visita a una casa de citas en la Narvarte," *El Universal*, August 21, 2015, www.eluniversal .com.mx/entrada-de-opinion/columna/ciro-gomez-leyva/nacion/2015/08/21/el -departamento-de-narvarte-era.

13. Carlos Marín, "DF: Opera o no el crimen organizado," *Milenio*, September 14, 2015, www.milenio.com/opinion/carlos-marin/el-asalto-la-razon/df-opera -o-no-el-crimen-organizado.

14. Coverage from the daily newspaper *La Razón* from August 2, 5, 6, 13, 17, 18, and 19, and September 1, 2, and 3, in 2015.

15. Indira Alfaro, "'Rubén y Nadia eran los más golpeados'. Nuevas revelaciones caso Narvarte," interview by Yuli García, *El Universal*, February 29, 2016, www .eluniversalvideo.com.mx/video/metropoli/2016/ruben-y-nadia-eran-los-mas -golpeados-nuevas-revelaciones-caso-narvarte.

16. "ONG denuncian filtraciones caso Narvarte," *El Universal*, August 6, 2015, www.eluniversal.com.mx/articulo/metropoli/df/2015/08/6/ong-denuncian -filtraciones-en-caso-narvarte.

17. "Jueza prohíbe a PGJDF difundir el caso," *La Razón*, September 2, 2015, www.razon.com.mx/ciudad/jueza-prohibe-a-pgjdf-difundir-el-caso.

18. "Detienen a funcionario de la PGJDF por filtrar caso Narvarte," *La Razón*, December 10, 2015, www.razon.com.mx/ciudad/detienen-a-funcionario-de-la-pgj df-por-filtrar-caso-narvarte.

19. "Huellas, fotos, videos, llamadas . . . inculpan a asesinos de la Narvarte," *La Raz*, February 1, 2015; "Con técnicas de EU, Canadá y Alemania PGJ resolvió el caso," *La Raz*, February 5, 2015.

20. Arturo Ángel, "Caso Narvarte: PGJDF concluye que amistad de detenidos con Mile fue el origen del crimen," *Animal Político*, November 27, 2015, www.animalpolitico.com/2015/11/caso-narvarte-sin-movil-pgjdf-concluye-que -amistad-de-detenidos-con-mile-fue-el-origen-del-crimen.

21. Salvador Camarena, "Esta es la declaración de Javier Duarte sobre los asesinatos en la colonia Narvarte," *Animal Político*, January 19, 2016, www.animalpolitico .com/2016/01/esta-es-la-declaracion-de-javier-duarte-sobre-los-asesinatos-en-la -colonia-narvarte.

22. "El gobernador de Veracruz se desvincula del asesinato del periodista Rubén Espinosa," *El Mundo*, August 12, 2015, www.elmundo.es/internacional /2015/08/12/55cb07afca47411d2d8b4579.html.

23. Juan Omar Fierro, "Empresas de seguridad de Arturo Bermúdez, ex jefe policiaco de Duarte, aún operan en la CDMX," *Aristegui Noticias*, February 6, 2017, aristeguinoticias.com/0602/mexico/empresas-de-seguridad-de-arturo-bermudez -ex-jefe-policiaco-de-duarte-aun-operan-en-la-cdmx.

24. "'Si iban por Mile, ¿por qué torturar a Nadia y Rubén?,'" *Aristegui Noticias*, August 2, 2016, aristeguinoticias.com/0208/mexico/si-iban-por-mile-por-que-tort urar-a-nadia-y-ruben.

25. Arturo Ángel, "Caso Narvarte: CDHDF enumera los errores e irregularidades cometidos en la investigación," *Animal Político*, June 22, 2017, www .animalpolitico.com/2017/06/narvarte-errores-investigacion-cdhdf.

26. Paris Martínez, "El comandante que investigó el multihomicidio en la Narvarte contaminó la escena del crimen," *Animal Político*, January 28, 2016, www .animalpolitico.com/2016/01/el-comandante-que-investigo-el-multihomicidio-en -la-narvarte-contamino-la-escena-del-crimen.

3: Moisés Sánchez

1. "Dan a conocer audio del momento del asesinato de Atilano Román," video, UNO TV, October 14, 2014, www.unotv.com/noticias/estados/noroeste/dan -a-conocer-audio-del-momento-del-asesinato-de-atilano-roman-796958; "Localizan sin vida a periodista en Sinaloa," *Animal Político*, October 23, 2014, www .animalpolitico.com/2014/10/noroeste.

2. Noé Zavaleta, "Subestima Duarte labor de reportero levantado: 'Es conductor de taxi y activista vecinal', dice," *Proceso*, January 3, 2015, www.proceso.com .mx/392100/subestima-duarte-labor-de-reportero-levantado-es-conductor-de-taxi -y-activista-vecinal-dice.

3. "Hallan el cuerpo del periodista mexicano José Moisés Sánchez," Univisión Noticias, January 26, 2015, YouTube video, www.youtube.com/watch?v=AJYDl _W8u4o.

4. "Declara Clemente Noé Rodríguez con subtítulos," January 25, 2015, YouTube video, www.youtube.com/watch?v=8RxJ1-sRmPs.

5. Secretariado Ejecutiva del Sistema Nacional de Seguridad Pública, "Incidencia delictiva del fuero común 2014," secretariadoejecutivo.gob.mx/docs/pdfs /estadisticas%20del%20fuero%20comun/Cieisp2014_092017.pdf.

6. CENCOS, Centro Nacional de Comunicación Social, is a nonprofit organization that provides communication services to social movements; see cencos.com .mx.

7. Manu Ureste, "Mientras Veracruz y Oaxaca 'se echan la bolita', SIP condena asesinato de periodista," *Animal Político*, May 6, 2015, www.animalpolitico .com/2015/05/veracruz-le-pasa-la-bolita-a-oaxaca-no-investigara-asesinato-del -periodista-armando-saldana.

8. Noé Zavaleta, "En Veracruz sólo hay robos de 'Frutsis y Pingüinos del Oxxo': Duarte," *Proceso*, October 14, 2014, www.proceso.com.mx/384800/en-veracruz -solo-hay-robos-de-frutsis-y-pinguinos-del-oxxo-duarte.

9. Omar Sánchez de Tagle, "El Sabueso: ¿Sólo se roban frutsis y pingüinos en Veracruz?" Animal Político, February 9, 2015, www.animalpolitico.com/elsabueso /el-sabueso-solo-se-roban-frutsis-y-pinguinos-en-veracruz.

10. "Informe Moisés Sánchez Cerezo. Undécimo periodista asesinado en Veracruz (periodo 2010–enero 2015)," report, Comisión Estatal para la Atención y Protección a Periodistas.

4: Pedro Canché

1. Elizabeth Rivera, "Diario de un preso de conciencia: Pedro Canché Herrera," Global Voices, es.globalvoices.org/2015/03/06/diario-de-un-preso-de-conciencia -pedro-canche-herrera.

2. Lydia Cacho, "Tulum: Tierra de ambiciones," Aristegui Noticias, September 7, 2015, aristeguinoticias.com/0709/mexico/tulum-tierra-de-ambiciones.

3. Pedro Canché, "Borge grita en El Renacer: 'Guardias desalojen al periodista'. Nadie le hace caso," Pedro Canché Noticias, June 10, 2017, pedrocanche.com/2017 /06/10/borge-grita-en-el-renacer-guardias-desalojen-al-periodista-nadie-le-hace -caso.

5: *Proceso*

1. Rafael Rodríguez Castañeda's time as director of *Proceso* ended on January 31, 2020, nearly twenty-one years after its beginning. His replacement is Jorge Carrasco, the reporter threatened by Javier Duarte. In a first-page editorial on February 9, it was stated that "this new generation" believes "that journalism goes beyond the mere telling of events and that its role is to contribute to democratic liberties." If this anticipates a more political view of journalism remains to be seen.

6: Along the Border

1. Marcela Turati, "San Fernando: El terror que jamás se ha ido," *Proceso*, August 31, 2016, www.proceso.com.mx/453016/san-fernando-terror-jamas-se-ha-ido.

2. Martín Moreno, "*NYT* y la prensa oficialista: Grupo Imagen, *La Razón*, *Excélsior*...," Sin Embargo, December 27, 2017, www.sinembargo.mx/27-12-2017 /3367288.

3. Holly Yan, "Which Nationalities Get Rejected the Most for US Asylum?" CNN.com, updated May 3, 2018, edition.cnn.com/2018/05/03/world/us-asylum -denial-rates-by-nationality/index.html.

4. Luis Carlos Sáinz, "20 años de impunidad del atentado a Blancornelas," *Zeta*, November 21, 2017, zetatijuana.com/2017/11/170826.

5. "Otra vez el CAF amenaza a Zeta," *Zeta*, April 8, 2017, zetatijuana.com/2017 /04/otra-vez-el-caf-amenaza-a-zeta.

7: Laura Castellanos

1. "Chocan versiones por muerte de 11," editorial in *Reforma*, January 7, 2015, https://www.reforma.com/aplicacioneslibre/preacceso/articulo/default.aspx ?id=433573&v=5&_ec_=1&urlredirect=https://www.reforma.com/aplicaciones /articulo/default.aspx?id=433573&v=5&_ec_=1; "México: Choques ponen en duda estrategia del gobierno," story by Alberto Arce on AP News, January 10, 2015, https://www.apnews.com/f15c6c19a5b04d2a959fe3a783929198.

2. Laura Castellanos, "Fueron los federales," Aristegui Noticias, April 19, 2015, aristeguinoticias.com/1904/mexico/fueron-los-federales.

3. Laura Castellanos, "Apatzingán: También fueron los militares," Aristegui Noticias, May 24, 2015, aristeguinoticias.com/2405/mexico/apatzingan-tambien -fueron-los-militares.

4. Laura Castellanos, "Masacre de Apatzingán: Los desplazados de Castillo," Aristegui Noticias, August 19, 2015, aristeguinoticias.com/1708/mexico/masacre -de-apatzingan-los-desplazados-de-castillo.

5. Cited in Carlos Fazio, *Estado de emergencia: De la guerra de Calderón a la guerra de Peña Nieto* (Mexico City: Grijalbo, 2016), 307.

6. Carlos Marín, "Apatzingán desde el anonimato," *Milenio Diario*, April 22, 2015, www.milenio.com/opinion/carlos-marin/el-asalto-la-razon/apatzingan-des de-el-anonimato.

7. Carlos Marín, interview by Adela Micha, *La Entrevista por Adela*, July 7, 2016, YouTube video, "Entrevista por Adela 07 Julio 2016 Carlos Marin y Julio Hernandez Astillero," youtu.be/OlwlXdt_nd8, 29:20.

8. "Discurso de Laura Castellanos, Premio Nacional de Periodismo 2015," September 21, 2016, www.periodismo.org.mx/assets/2015_Discurso_Castellanos .pdf.

8: Carmen Aristegui

1. Daniel Lizárraga et al., *La casa blanca de Peña Nieto* (Mexico City: Grijalbo, 2015).

2. Unidad de Investigaciones Especiales, "Licitación Tren México-Querétaro: '¿Cual es la prisa?,'" Aristegui Noticias, October 24, 2014, aristeguinoticias.com

/2410/mexico/prisa-por-licitar-tren-mexico-queretaro-inhibio-competencia-entre
-constructoras.

3. Sebastián Barragán, "Videgaray dirigió a China en propuesta del Tren
México-Querétaro, revela documento," Aristegui Noticias, February 6, 2018, ari
steguinoticias.com/0602/mexico/videgaray-dirigio-a-china-en-propuesta-del-tren
-mexico-queretaro-revela-documento/.

4. Unidad de Investigaciones Especiales, "Va un solo competidor por Tren
México-Querétaro; es cercano a EPN," Aristegui Noticias, October 16, 2014,
aristeguinoticias.com/1610/mexico/va-un-solo-competidor-por-tren-mexico
-queretaro-es-cercano-a-epn.

5. "EPN frena el tren México-Querétaro; revoca licitación, por 'dudas e
inquietudes,'" Aristegui Noticias, November 7, 2014, aristeguinoticias.com
/0711/mexico/epn-para-el-tren-mexico-queretaro-revoca-licitacion-por-dudas
-e-inquietudes.

6. Sebastián Barragán, "China reclama a México 11 mil millones por cancelación
del Tren México-Querétaro," Aristegui Noticias, November 22, 2017, aristeguino
ticias.com/2211/mexico/china-reclama-a-mexico-11-mil-millones-por-cancelacion
-del-tren-mexico-queretaro.

7. Angélica Rivera, "Precisiones sobre la propiedad Sierra Gorda 150 - Sra.
Angélica Rivera de Peña," November 18, 2014, YouTube video, youtu.be/tdJ-
06CLjjxE.

8. Kate del Castillo, "Kate del Castillo habla de la polémica carta que le envió a
'El Chapo,'" interview by Carmen Aristegui, Aristegui, CNN en Español, November 9, 2015, cnnespanol.cnn.com/video/cnnee-intvw-aristegui-kate-del-castillo-33
-miners.

9. "Explicación de Angélica Rivera 'convence poco', señala encuesta," SDP Noticias, November 22, 2014, www.sdpnoticias.com/nacional/2014/11/22/explica
cion-de-angelica-rivera-convence-poco-senala-encuesta; "Perciban conflicto des
interés con 'Casa Blanca,'" Encuestas, un blog de Grupo Reforma, November 22,
2014, gruporeforma-blogs.com/encuestas/?p=5129.

10. Wilbert Torre, El despido (Mexico City: Temas de Hoy, 2015), 111.

11. Enrique Sánchez, "Peña Nieto nombra a Virgilio Andrade como secretario de
la Función Pública," Excélsior, February 3, 2015, www.excelsior.com.mx/nacional
/2015/02/03/1006280.

12. "MVS Radio no acepta el ultimátum de Carmen Aristegui," MVS Noticias,
March 15, 2015, mvsnoticias.com/noticias/nacionales/mvs-radio-no-acepta-el-ulti
matum-de-carmen-aristegui-914.

13. Nicolás Lucas, "¿Puede sobrevivir MVS Comunicaciones sin Carmen Aristegui?," El Economista, March 18, 2015, www.eleconomista.com.mx/empresas
/Puede-sobrevivir-MVS-Comunicaciones-sin-Carmen-Aristegui-20150318-0050
.html.

14. Nathaniel Parish Flannery, "Firing of Dissident Journalist Carmen Aristegui Bad News for Mexico," forbes.com, March 16, 2015, www.forbes.com/sites

/nathanielparishflannery/2015/03/16/firing-of-dissident-journalist-carmen
-aristegui-bad-news-for-mexico/#61a7551366e3.

15. Associated Press, "Mexican journalist fired; had revealed presidential scandal," *Dhaka Tribune*, March 17, 2015, www.dhakatribune.com/uncategorized
/2015/03/17/mexican-journalist-fired-had-revealed-presidential-scandal.

16. Petition #EnDefensaDeAristegui on change.org, www.change.org/p/car
men-aristegui-por-la-libertad-de-expresi%C3%B3n-en-la-prensa-mexicana-a-que
-juntamos-100-mil-firmas-endefensadearistegui.

17. "Alianza MÉXICOLEAKS rechaza la decision de MVS de dar por terminada
la relación laboral con la periodista Carmen Aristegui y su equipo editorial," Periodistas de a Pie, March 17, 2015, periodistasdeapie.org.mx/posicionamiento-20
.php.

18. "Aristegui pide a MVS regresar al aire; 'nuestra relación ha terminado',
responde la empresa," Animal Político, March 20, 2015, www.animalpolitico.com
/2015/03/aristegui-pide-a-mvs-regresar-al-aire-para-seguir-haciendo-periodismo.

19. Carmen Aristegui, "Aristegui: la censura y el despido, por presión de Los
Pinos," interview by Jenaro Villamil, *Proceso*, March 21, 2015, www.proceso.com
.mx/399065/399065-aristegui-la-censura-y-el-despido-por-presion-de-los-pinos.

20. Statement by the President of the Republic of Mexico, November 10, 2014,
http://www.presidencia.gob.mx/wp-content/uploads/2014/11/Sierra-Gorda
-nota-informativa.pdf.

21. Isaín Mandujano, "En la administración de Peña Nieto se duplicaron
agresiones contra periodistas," *Proceso*, March 24, 2015, www.proceso.com.mx
/?p=399259.

22. During the legal petition campaign, proposed initially by attorney Roberto
Hernández and producer Laura Barranco, the San Borja Group was comprised of
Blanche Petrich, Aurelio Fernández, Lorenzo Meyer, Laura Barranco, Fabrizio
Mejía Madrid, Rafael Pineda "Rapé," Enrique Galván Ochoa, Oriol Malló, Héctor
Bonilla, Denise Dresser, Jenaro Villamil, Ernesto Ledesma, Manuel de Santiago,
Teresa Cristo, Mardonio Carballo, Alberto Escorcia, Adriana Buentello, Ameyalli
Motta, and myself. We had the support of attorneys Karla Micheel Salas, David
Peña, and Carlos Meza.

23. "Atacan Aristegui Noticias; el sitio, caído varias horas," Aristegui Noticias,
April 19, 2015, aristeguinoticias.com/1904/mexico/atacan-aristegui-noticias-el
-sitio-caido-varias-horas.

24. Ricardo Alemán, "Con Peña Nieto, la mayor libertad de expression," *Milenio
Diario*, September 12, 2016, www.milenio.com/opinion/ricardo-aleman/itinera
rio-politico/con-pena-nieto-la-mayor-libertad-de-expresion.

25. "Video: Opera #RedProstitución en PRI-DF (investigación)," Aristegui Noticias, April 2, 2014, aristeguinoticias.com/0204/mexico/opera-redprostitucion-en
-pri-df-investigacion-mvs.

26. Ciro Gómez Leyva, "Opinión sobre salida de Carmen Aristegui de MVS," *Por
la mañana*, March 16, 2015, YouTube video, youtu.be/vfVj813uEN0.

27. Memo DGCS/NI: 44/2015 from the Federal Judicial Authority, April 15, 2015, www.cjf.gob.mx/documentos/notasInformativas/docsNotasInformativas /2015/notaInformativa44.pdf.

28. José Roldán Xopa, "El amparo Aristegui vs MVS," *La Silla Rota*, April 16, 2015, lasillarota.com/opinion/columnas/el-amparo-aristegui-vs-mvs/77691.

29. Lizárraga et al., *La casa blanca de Peña Nieto*, 31–32.

30. "Seis meses necesitó Función Pública para exonerar a Peña, Rivera y Videgaray," Animal Político, August 21, 2015, www.animalpolitico.com/2015/08/epn -angelica-rivera-y-luis-videgaray-no-incurrieron-en-conflicto-de-intereses-virgilio -andrade.

31. Mauricio Rubí, "EPN: Reconozco que cometí un error," *El Economista*, July 28, 2020, www.eleconomista.com.mx/politica/EPNReconozco-que-cometi -un-error-20160718-0073.html.

32. "Aristegui denuncia acoso judicial por investigación de la casa blanca," Aristegui Noticias, July 21, 2016, www.youtube.com/watch?v=ZBm1zBhe1SY.

33. "Difunde Presidencia lista de empresas y periodistas que tuvieron contratos con gobierno de EPN," Animal Político, May 23, 2019, www.animalpolitico.com /2019/05/periodistas-empresas-contratos-gobierno-epn.

34. "Campaña de desprestigio y amenazas contra Carmen Aristegui en redes," Aristegui Noticias, November 23, 2016, aristeguinoticias.com/2311/mexico /campana-de-desprestigio-y-amenazas-contra-carmen-aristegui-en-redes.

35. "Allanan redacción de Aristegui Noticias y sustraen computadora de Investigaciones Especiales," Aristegui Noticias, November 23, 2016, aristeguinoticias.com /2311/mexico/allanan-redaccion-de-aristegui-noticias-y-sustraen-computadora-de -investigaciones-especiales.

36. "Tres sujetos allanan las instalaciones de Proceso," *Proceso*, May 26, 2017, www.proceso.com.mx/488351/tres-sujetos-allanan-las-instalaciones-proceso -video.

37. Lizárraga et al., *La casa blanca de Peña Nieto*, 15.

38. "Siguen cortando lenguas: Aristegui al recibir Premio Knight (Video y discurso)," Aristegui Noticias, November 16, 2016, aristeguinoticias.com/1611/mexico /siguen-cortando-lenguas-aristegui-al-recibir-premio-knight-video-y-discurso.

39. "Siguen cortando lenguas: Aristegui al recibir Premio Knight."

9: Javier Valdez

1. Alejandra Guillén, Mago Torres, and Marcela Turati, "El país de las 2 mil fosas," Pie de Página, November 12, 2018, piedepagina.mx/el-pais-de-las-2-mil -fosas.

2. Javier Valdez Cárdenas, *Periodismo escrito con sangre: Antología periodistica: Textos que ninguna bala podrá callar* (Mexico City: Aguilar, 2017), 229, 232.

3. "¿Quiénes somos?" *Ríodoce*, riodoce.mx/quiene-somos.

4. Juan Antonio Fernández Velázquez, "Breve historia social del narcotráfico en Sinaloa," *Revista Digital Universitaria* 11, no. 8 (August 1, 2010): 6, www.revista.unam.mx/vol.11/num8/art82/art82.pdf.

5. "'No disparé a los Guzmán y soy amigo del "Mayo" Zambada': Dámaso," *Ríodoce*, February 20, 2017, riodoce.mx/narcotrafico-2/no-dispare-a-los-guzman -y-soy-amigo-del-mayo-zambada-damaso.

6. Miroslava Breach, "Impone el crimen organizado candidatos a ediles en Chihuahua," *La Jornada*, March 4, 2016, La Jornada. March 4, 2016.

7. Javier Valdez (@jvrvaldez), "A Miroslava la mataron por lengua larga. Que nos maten a todos, si esa es la condena de muerte por reportear este infierno. No al silencio.," Twitter, March 25, 2017, twitter.com/jvrvaldez/status /845656653563396098.

8. Javier Valdez, *Narcoperiodismo: La prensa en medio del crimen y la denucia* (Mexico City: Aguilar, 2016), 18–19.

10: The End of the Telenovela

1. Azan Ahmed, "A Journalist Was Killed in Mexico. Then His Colleagues Were Hacked," *New York Times*, November 27, 2018, www.nytimes.com/es/2018 /11/27/javier-valdez-riodoce-pegasus.

2. Claudia Altamirano, "Usan Pegasus y sitios falsos de Animal Político y Proceso para espiar a la viuda de Javier Valdez," Animal Político, March 20, 2019, www .animalpolitico.com/2019/03/espionaje-griselda-triana-viuda-javier-valdez.

3. Azam Ahmed and Nicole Perlroth, "Using Texts as Lures, Government Spyware Targets Mexican Journalists and Their Families," *New York Times*, June 19, 2017, www.nytimes.com/es/2017/06/19/mexico-pegasus-nso-group-espionaje.

4. Francisco Resendiz, "EPN: Nos sentimos espiados, yo mismo, como presidente?" *El Universal*, June 22, 2017.

5. "La estafa maestra," Animal Político, September 5, 2017, www.animalpolitico .com/estafa-maestra/index.html.

6. María Amparo Casar and Luis Carlos Ugalde, *Dinero bajo la mesa: Financiamiento y gasto ilegal de campañas políticas en México* (Mexico City: Integralia Consultores y Mexicanos Contra la Corrupción y la Impunidad, 2018), 157–68, dinerobajolamesa.org/wp-content/uploads/2018/05/Dinero-Bajo-la-Mesa. -Financiamiento-y-Gasto-Ilegal-de-las-Campa%C3%B1as-en-M%C3%A9xico .pdf.

7. Paulina Castaño, *Contar "lo bueno" cuesta mucho: El gasto en publicidad oficial del gobierno federal de 2013 a 2016* (Mexico City: Fundar Centro de Análisis e Investigación, 2017), fundar.org.mx/mexico/pdf/P.O.2013-2016oK2.pdf.

8. Azam Ahmed, "Using Billions in Cash, Mexico Controls News Media," *New York Times*, December 25, 2017, www.nytimes.com/2017/12/25/world/americas/mexico-press-government-advertising.html.

9. "Colectivo #MediosLibres exige al Legislativo atender la regulación de la Publicidad Oficial en tiempo y forma," Article 19 México, February 7, 2018, articulo19.org/colectivo-medioslibres-exige-al-legislativo-atender-la-regulacion-de-la-publicidad-oficial-en-tiempo-y-forma.

10. "Legislativo incumple con la sentencia de la Suprema Corte sobre regulación de publicidad official," Article 19 México, April 26, 2018, articulo19.org/legislativo-incumple-con-la-sentencia-de-la-suprema-corte-sobre-regulacion-de-publicidad-oficial.

11. Red #RompeElMiedo, "Elecciones 2018," (Mexico City: Red #RompeEl Miedo, 2018), informaterompeelmiedo.mx/wp-content/uploads/2018/10/RRM-informe-elecciones-2018.pdf.

12. Alberto Molina, "Sexenio de Peña Nieto cierra con una aprobación de 24%," *El Economista*, November 22, 2018, www.eleconomista.com.mx/politica/Sexenio-de-Pena-Nieto-cierra-con-una-aprobacion-de-24-20181122-0182.html.

11: The Beginning of a New Regime

1. Lydia Cacho, *Los demonios del Edén* (De Bolsillo: México, 2005).

2. Blanche Petrich, "'Mi gober, tú eres el héroe': Kamel Nacif a Mario Marín," *La Jornada*, February 14, 2006, https://www.jornada.com.mx/2006/02/14/index.php?section=politica&article=005n1pol.

3. Petrich, "'Mi gober, tú eres el héroe.'"

4. Signa_Lab ITESO, "Democracia, libertad de expresión y esfera digital: Análisis de tendencias y tipologías en Twitter: El caso de #RedAMLOVE," Signa_Lab, February 28, 2019, signalab.iteso.mx/informes/informe_redamlove.html.

5. Ricardo Raphael, "El intelectual imperial," *Proceso*, April 7, 2019, www.proceso.com.mx/579395/el-intelectual-imperial.

6. Raphael, "El intelectual imperial."

ABOUT THE AUTHOR

Témoris Grecko is a Mexican journalist and political scientist who has worked in ninety-four countries and territories and has completed three round-the-world trips. His interviews show "Diametral" broadcasts Saturdays on TV UNAM, the National University channel. A regular contributor to *Proceso, Aristegui Noticias,* and other media outlets, he has published five books in Spanish: on the Mexican Catholic far right movements, racism and AIDS in Southern and Eastern Africa, the 2009 uprisings in Iran, the Syrian civil war, and the crimes against Ayotzinapa students and the following phony official investigation. He has made two feature film documentaries, *Watching Them Die: The Mexican Army and the 43 Disappeared* (available free: youtu.be /p9709TuNen0) and *The Truth Shall Not Be Killed* (available on free loan for non-profit public screenings, trailer youtu .be/ywvbpW2KKj0), and is a founding member of Ojos de Perro vs la Impunidad (odpmx.org), Frontline Freelance Register, and Red por la Libertad de Expresión y contra la Violencia a Comunicadores. He is currently based in Mexico City, working on a project to improve the safety and quality of journalism in his country.

temoris.org
fb.me/temoris (Spanish)
fb.me/TemorisJournalist (English)
instagram.com/temoris
twitter.com/temoris

PUBLISHING IN THE PUBLIC INTEREST

Thank you for reading this book published by The New Press. The New Press is a nonprofit, public interest publisher. New Press books and authors play a crucial role in sparking conversations about the key political and social issues of our day.

We hope you enjoyed this book and that you will stay in touch with The New Press. Here are a few ways to stay up to date with our books, events, and the issues we cover:

- Sign up at www.thenewpress.com/subscribe to receive updates on New Press authors and issues and to be notified about local events
- Like us on Facebook: www.facebook.com /newpressbooks
- Follow us on Twitter: www.twitter.com/thenewpress
- Follow us on Instagram: www.instagram.com/thenew press

Please consider buying New Press books for yourself; for friends and family; or to donate to schools, libraries, community centers, prison libraries, and other organizations involved with the issues our authors write about.

The New Press is a 501(c)(3) nonprofit organization. You can also support our work with a tax-deductible gift by visiting www.thenewpress.com/donate.